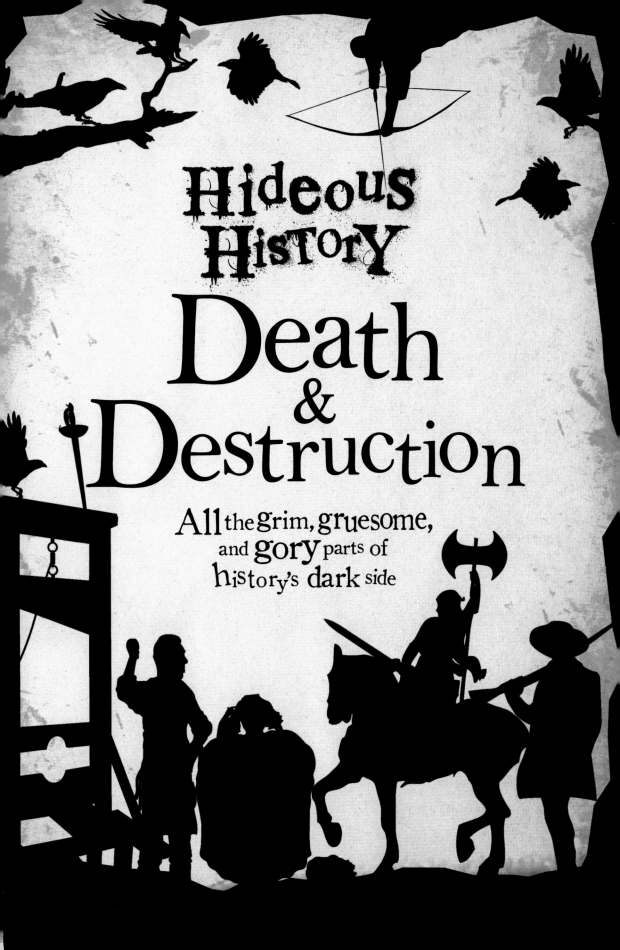

Hideous History

Death & Destruction

All the grim, gruesome, and gory parts of history's dark side

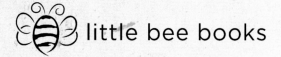

A division of Bonnier Publishing
853 Broadway, New York, New York 10003

Manufactured in China 024

First Edition

2 4 6 8 10 9 7 5 3 1

Library of Congress Cataloging-in-Publication Data
is available upon request.

ISBN 978-1-4998-0082-1

littlebeebooks.com

bonnierpublishing.com

Hideous History

Death & Destruction

All the grim, gruesome, and gory parts of history's dark side

Sandra Lawrence

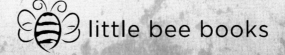 little bee books

CONTENTS

5

Death & Destruction

There are many causes of murder and death. It's possible there are as many reasons why people kill as there are people killed. There are almost as many ways to die too, all of them horrible—some more horrible than others. One or two are so terrible that you wonder how a human could even think them up.

Death can come in the heat of battle; in a single moment of anger; or from cold, hard calculation. Murder has even been a traditional way for rulers to get rid of their rivals, often within their own families. Great leaders manage to dream up some absolutely terrifying methods of execution, but at the end of the day, someone has to actually do the dirty deed.

Professional executioners have traditionally lived on the outskirts of society, often handing the "trade" down from father to son. Most see it as a necessary evil, though some of the most notorious have enjoyed their work just a little too much.

Serial killers are rare, thankfully. Sadly, there are still far too many to mention in this book, but even they kill for different reasons. Some believe voices—or even God—told them to do it, some had awful things done to them as a child, some do it for the sheer sadistic kick, and some.... well, we still have no idea what on earth made them do it.

Whatever the reason, whatever the murder, it leads to a feeling of fear and horror in a community, and occasionally, to mayhem and destruction.

Ever had one of those giggling fits in class? You know—the kid across the aisle starts laughing, and the one next to him catches it? You find yourself cracking a smile, too. Then your neighbor bursts out laughing. The teacher tells you to STOP IT! *NOW!*—and you know you must, but you just can't. There isn't even anything particularly funny, but everyone's giggling like crazy. Soon, the whole class is snorting and snickering. Next thing you know, you're lined up outside the principal's office, wondering what on earth just happened.

It's simple—it was a very mild case of mass hysteria. Mayhem happens in all societies. Some of it is just an extreme version of classroom giggles, where entire groups of people start doing something they can't stop, and it goes on for days, weeks, or even months as those around them get very worried.

Sometimes madness and destruction can lead to rebellion, or even all-out revolution, ending in a regime change for a country or even a continent. It could be the result of discontentment in society, often sparked by a charismatic speaker or leader. Sometimes a religious aspect is involved—people can find personal passion, or a ritual leads everyone who's taking part in it to be swept into a frenzy. The Aztecs, for example, whipped themselves into a mania of death, slaughtering thousands of humans as sacrifices, fueled by drinking chocolate!

People put forward possible explanations for individual explosions of madness and destruction—epidemics of strange diseases, for example. One popular theory is a disease called ergot poisoning, which is caused by a kind of mold that grows on cereal crops in wet years and can lead to convulsions and gangrene. It's been suggested the seizures experienced by the "witches" in Salem, Massachusetts, may have been due to ergotism.

Madness and destruction can find its roots in cold, hard cash, too. The South Sea Bubble in England in the early eighteenth century saw otherwise sensible people clamoring to buy what turned out to be worthless shares of stock in the company. One or two made their fortune; the rest lost everything, wondering how on earth they'd managed to get suckered in.

In this book we'll look at a whole range of both murder and mayhem. Sometimes the two can't be separated—destruction leads to death and sometimes death leads to destruction. We can't even begin to figure out why people do dreadful things to each other, but maybe, just maybe, if we know about it, we can stop it from happening again.

BOUDICA

Seventeen years since the Romans invaded Britannia, and the Celtic tribes were fuming....

Boudica gathered support from the Iceni tribespeople.

Up in East Anglia, King Prasutagus was allowed to rule his Iceni tribe as a puppet "client king"—as long as he pledged allegiance to Rome and paid heavy taxes. The invaders lent him money, too, but Iron Age Britons didn't really understand the idea of loans. Their society was based on bartering and gifts, and Prasutagus assumed the money was a present from the nice, kind Romans. He and his wife, Boudica, and their two daughters enjoyed thirteen years of peaceful rule.

When Prasutagus died in 60 CE, he left half of his land to his daughters and the other half to the Roman Emperor Nero.

The Romans were outraged. How dare he leave Nero just half? And the rest to *girls*?

Furious, they called in their loans. Boudica couldn't—or wouldn't—pay, so the kingdom was pillaged. Iceni chieftains were stripped of their estates, and the king's relatives were enslaved.

Boudica herself was stripped and beaten. Her daughters were assaulted. Even Tacitus, the Roman historian who recorded it all, was shocked.

He wasn't as shocked as the Iceni people, though. Taxed to pay for the cost of their own invasion, they were already enraged. Boudica was the angriest of all, and under her leadership, a disorganized mob gained momentum.

They were joined by the tribe next door, the Trinovantes, who were also extremely angry. Their city, Camulodunum, named for Camulus, the god of war, had been hijacked by the Romans to be *their* capital city. The conquerors forced the Trinovantes to build a temple to worship Emperor Claudius, the very man who'd invaded them seventeen years ago.

The rebel army headed for Camulodunum, modern-day Colchester. The Roman army was away, busy supressing the Druids in Wales. The city was undefended. The Britons streamed in, looting, killing, and burning. Hundreds of terrified citizens headed for the temple of Claudius and locked themselves inside, waiting for rescue.

It wasn't coming. Boudica had already wiped out 1,500 of the Ninth Legion's 2,000 soldiers on the way. The bloodthirsty Britons smashed the temple's roof tiles and leapt onto the people inside, butchering every man, woman, and child. They spent the night feasting in the acrid smoke of the burning city.

News spread fast. The people of Londinium had an uneasy feeling they were next. Some were able to flee, burying their valuables first; most didn't. The Roman historian Cassius Dio describes the Celtic rebels stringing up naked nobles, chopping parts off and even skewering women with sharp sticks from end to end. They then made sacrifices to the gods and partied some more.

The queen of the Iceni wasn't done yet. She figured Verulamium, today's St. Albans, was ripe for the picking. The tide was turning, though. Her warriors were busy feasting, and their wagons were weighed down with all their loot. They were getting sloppy, and unbeknownst to them, the Roman commander Gaius Suetonius Paulinus was marching his troops south.

By the time the rebels raided Verulamium, its citizens had fled, taking their valuables with them. Finding little to plunder, the angry mob attacked outlying farms and villas.

We don't know where the final "Battle of Watling Street" took place—the road is 276 miles long, and every historian has their own opinion. According to history, Boudica stood in her chariot and gave a long, stirring speech, but it was all in vain. The Romans' clever tactics funneled the Britons into a sea of spears. Boudica probably took her own life, with poison.

Tacitus boasts 80,000 Britons died to just 400 legionnaires. Modern estimates reckon it was more likely 40,000 Brits and 1,000 centurions, but that's still a lot of bodies that presumably still lie somewhere between London and the city of Wroxeter in the north, still waiting to be discovered!

Boudica's army attacked the Temple of Claudius and burned it to the ground.

9

Scary Iron Age Queen

Medieval scribes made a mistake with Boudica's name, accidentally calling her Boadicea. *Bouda* is Celtic for "victory," so Boudica is probably the Iron Age equivalent of Victoria.

British tribes were familiar with having the occasional female ruler, but the Romans didn't get it at all. They thought women should stay at home and look nice, not tell men what to do! Imagine how embarrassed they were when they had to admit to the folks back home that not only had their troops been defeated by hairy barbarians, but they'd been beaten by a GIRL!

Roman historians made Boudica sound really scary so that it wouldn't seem so bad that an entire Roman legion had been beaten by her.

The writer Cassius Dio describes her as terrifying, with fierce eyes, a harsh voice, and a mane of wild red hair, which was probably dyed with a substance called henna. She had a colorful tunic, a thick cloak with a brooch, and a golden torque necklace. Several ancient torques have been dug up by archaeologists. Maybe one belonged to Boudica!

A Roman soldier wearing full armor attacks with a gladius.

Weapons

The Romans were battle-hardened and well-trained. They also had a lot of gear. Centurions had armor made from iron and leather, wore strong helmets, and carried large rectangular shields called "scutums," decorated in red and silver. A soldier would wield a long "pilum," or spear, that stuck into an opponent's shield to make it useless, along with a short "gladius," or double-edged sword, designed to stab, slash, and twist into an enemy's flesh.

Some of Boudica's army had powerful weapons, but most weren't soldiers and had to use whatever they could lay their hands on, from farm implements to hunting knives.

Bad Omens

The Romans were very superstitious, and tales of omens predicting Boudica's uprising were reported. In Camulodunum the statue of Victory mysteriously toppled over. It was said that old women in the street started raving in a strange language, ghostly laughter was heard in the air, and in the theater, people reported eerie howling and wailing.

Miles away in the Thames estuary, soothsayers saw visions of a ransacked town reflected in the water, and it was said the seas turned the color of blood.

A Family Business

The Iceni brought their families and possessions along with them to battle, but it wasn't for a nice vacation. From Grandma to baby, valuable gold jewelry to pots and pans, everything was trundled along in carts beside them because they figured they'd be safer together. It slowed them down, but the tribesfolk feared their loved ones could be robbed, attacked, or killed if they were left at home. The families watched the battle as if it were some kind of weird sporting event!

Though Boudica's chariot probably didn't have spikes on the wheels, her statue near Westminster Pier shows her riding in one.

PLATFORM 9¾

Harry Potter's Next-Door Neighbor?

A legend arose in the last century that Boudica is buried under Platform 9 at King's Cross Station in London. Sadly, there isn't any evidence for it, otherwise she'd be snuggled up to Platform 9¾ where the *Hogwarts Express* terminates!

Her chariot wheels probably didn't have knives on them, either. They were the invention of a sculptor, Thomas Thorneycroft, for his famous statue of Boudica and her daughters outside the Houses of Parliament in Westminster.

How Much Is True?

For centuries the story of Boudica was assumed to be a nice myth about a warrior queen, but about as realistic as tales of King Arthur and his knights.

As the science of archaeology began to emerge in the late nineteenth century, new discoveries began to imply that the Roman historians might actually be (broadly) telling the truth.

A thin layer of soil, scorched red from being burned at very high temperature, was discovered underneath modern-day Colchester and London. It was found to be exactly the right period: 60 or 61 CE. The ruins of Claudius's temple were unearthed in the foundations of Colchester castle.

Even more extraordinarily, a small boy swimming in the Alde river in 1907 found a decapitated head from a statue, clearly hacked off with violence. He painted it white and displayed it in his garden, but it's now believed to be Claudius, looted from the temple by Boudica's army and thrown into the water as a sacrifice. It's now in the British Museum in London.

VLAD DRACULA

WALLACHIA (MODERN-DAY ROMANIA), 1431–1476

The original Dracula, far scarier than any vampire....

In 1456, after having waged war on everyone, including his own family, Vlad Dracula sat on the blood-soaked throne of Wallachia. He'd been there once before, and he'd rule, briefly, again, but this would be his longest, most active—and his cruelest—reign.

He got rid of his unfaithful nobles and created a new aristocracy from his peasant soldiers. Under Vlad's rule there were very low levels of crime, immorality, and laziness. There was a good reason for this. Vlad "the Impaler" went for the jugular, though not always in the most direct route. In a courtyard full of bodies on spikes, townspeople lost the appetite for bribery, corruption, laziness, or theft.

That's not to say Dracula didn't like other "punishments." Victims were skinned alive, burned, and had parts cut off them. If anyone

Looks Aren't Everything

In the fifteenth century, a weird Austrian archduke, Ferdinand II, collected pictures of people with physical deformities. They included a man born without arms or legs, hairy-faced "wolf-children," and even a man whose eye had been pierced by a lance and lived with the weapon sticking out of his head.

Ferdinand also collected paintings of tyrants and villains, and the only "proper" portrait of Vlad Dracula still lives in Castle Ambras's Cabinet of Curiosities. Vlad's bloodshot eyes, protruding lip, long curly hair, and giant moustache look gaudy next to his furs, jewels, and silks, but the picture wasn't meant to flatter. Painted a century after Vlad's death, it was intended to show him as a depraved despot.

Lurid woodcuts of Vlad feasting among forests of dead bodies on sticks come from pamphlets printed just after his death. At one point it even became fashionable for biblical paintings depicting the martyrdom of Saint Andrew to include Dracula lurking in the background enjoying the spectacle!

Count Dracula

We can be pretty sure Vlad Dracula was not a vampire, though legends insist he dipped his bread in victims' blood. There have been vampire myths across the world since ancient times, but Count Dracula the vampire was an invention of the Victorian novelist Bram Stoker.

Stoker certainly knew of Vlad III, though, and the fictional Count Dracula talks of his battle with the Turks and betrayal by his brother, just like the real fifteenth-century Vlad Dracula.

Vlad had the turbans of Turkish envoys nailed to their heads.

confronted him, he'd have their whole village destroyed. People felt they'd been let off lightly if they'd merely been decapitated. The usually powerful medieval church was cowed into submission, with monks impaled on the spot for even suggesting he might be getting a little extreme.

There was a catch, though, even for Dracula. He was expected to pay tribute to Constantinople, now Istanbul. Ten thousand gold ducats every year. Presented in person. Oh, and he had to kiss the hem of the Sultan's coat. Unsurprisingly the ducats went unpaid and the Sultan's hem unsmooched.

Envoys arrived from Constantinople, demanding the ducats, kisses—and 500 Wallachian boy recruits for the Turkish army. The meeting didn't go well. Vlad took exception to the ambassadors "not removing their hats"—and nailed their turbans onto their heads.

The sultan invaded, with Vlad's brother Radu leading the ranks. Dracula was forced to retreat, but he didn't go quietly. Villages were burned, crops were torched, and wells were poisoned. Anyone in the way saw the pointy end of a stake. When the Ottoman army arrived at a narrow pass, they were sickened by an unusual "forest"—20,000 dead or dying ambushed Turks skewered like kebabs.

Of course, Vlad hardly coddled his own troops. After one battle he inspected his men. Anyone wounded at the front was rewarded. Anyone wounded from behind was impaled.

Eventually the sheer size of the Turkish army forced Vlad Dracula to the Transylvanian Alps. Romance tells of valiant escape attempts—of secret passages, horses shoed backwards, and heroic ascents across mountain peaks—but all was in vain.

Radu the Handsome now ruled Wallachia. Held captive, Vlad bided his time for twelve years, impaling mice and small birds to keep himself amused while he waited for his chance....

Vlad Dracula

Dracula's father was betrayed by his own boyars (nobles), taken captive, and assassinated, and then his older brother was blinded with a red-hot poker and buried alive. A Hungarian ruler called Hunyadi filled the king-shaped hole in Wallachia, now part of Romania. The Ottoman Turks didn't like Hunyadi and thought they could easily manipulate young Vlad if they helped him take the throne instead.

While the Turkish army occupied the new king abroad, Vlad quietly took the throne. Everyone was so surprised that there wasn't even a battle. He was around seventeen years old.

Vlad knew it couldn't last, but he reckoned the Ottomans would back him up. Unfortunately, the victorious Turks had not only failed to chase the Hungarians to make sure they were beaten, but they'd stayed on the battlefield and set tables to feast among the vanquished dead, an old Ottoman tradition. Hunyadi, down but not out, came home and whooped Vlad's butt.

Vlad went off to Moldavia to lick his wounds. It would be many years before he became *voivode* (prince) for a second time. Vlad's third rule, twenty years later, was even shorter—not even two months.

None of the many stories of Vlad Dracula's death are proven, and more theories come up all the time. According to some, he was decapitated, and his head sent to Constantinople preserved in honey to prove he was dead. It was displayed, appropriately, on a spike. For years his headless body was supposed to lie at Snagov Monastery, but when his "grave" was opened, it was empty. . . .

The emblem of the Order of the Dragon.

Dragon, Devil, Stake

Although in modern Romanian, *Drac* means "devil," most historians agree Vlad's official surname has more "heroic" origins.

Vlad's dad was also Vlad—Vlad "Dracul." He belonged to the chivalric knights' Order of the Dragon, formed to defend the cross against the enemies of Christianity. In the fifteenth century, that meant the Ottoman Turks. The word *Dracula* basically means "Son of the Dragon."

Actually, Vlad's other name, Tepes, which doesn't sound half as scary, is far more sinister. It means "stake" in Romanian, a reference to Vlad Junior's favorite hobby.

Castle Dracula

When he first came to power, Dracula ruled from his palace at Târgoviste, where most of his worst atrocities are said to have taken place.

He hated the Wallachian aristocrats, called boyars, who had betrayed his father and older brother. He set about exterminating them, but cruelly, he impaled only the women and children. He saved the men, whom he turned into slaves, and forced them to rebuild his favorite citadel.

Close to the Transylvanian border, Castle Poenari was remote, eerie, and inaccessible, a perfect fortress built by Dracula's former nobles with their bare hands. Locals still whisper of a secret passage leading down through a cave to the banks of the Arges River and point to a perilous sheer drop from the castle walls where they say Vlad's wife flung herself to her death rather than be captured by the Turks.

Choose Your Weapon

Historians believe between 40,000 and 100,000 people were killed by Vlad Dracula. In one letter, Vlad boasted of a chillingly exact 23,884 dead, not counting the ones whose heads were cut off or who died as their homes burned. The letter was accompanied by sacks containing a bunch of heads, noses, and ears.

With killing on such an industrial scale, he had to be prepared. Empty stakes lived in every public square, meeting place, and palace courtyard, carefully rounded at the end so you didn't die too quickly and coated in oil for a good slide.

Not everyone was staked from the buttocks up. Some were dropped onto stakes through secret trap doors. Spikes might spear through the heart, head, stomach, or chest. Variety was the spice of death.

Dracula might have taken impalement to a whole new level, but he didn't invent it. It was known in antiquity, and the Ottoman Turks practiced the torture widely.

A secret trap door hides a pit of stakes.

Tall Tales

It's hard to know just how much of Vlad Dracula's history is true. After his death, the newly invented printing press was hungry for juicy gossip. The gorier the story, the more money the pamphleteers made. News sheets had him blinding, strangling, boiling, skinning, roasting, hacking, nailing, stabbing, and burying his victims alive.

It could be true. Vlad happily admitted to a lot of sadistic atrocities. His enemies, however, had good reason to make him out to be evil incarnate, and we'll never know how much "history" is actually exaggeration.

Some folk tales, however, depict him as a hero. Many people even today will tell you Dracula was harsh but fair, defended Romania from the Ottomans, and saved the country from corruption.

Blood Brothers

As children, Vlad and his half-brother Radu were sent to the fortress of Egrigöz ("Crooked Eyes") as hostages of the Ottoman sultan. They were treated well, schooled in Turkish, logic, and the Quran. They also learned warfare and horsemanship, which to modern eyes, seems an odd thing to teach your enemy.

Young Vlad was not a model prisoner. Impudent and defiant, he was bad-tempered and jealous of his goody-goody little brother, Radu "the Handsome," who was the Sultan's favorite. The only thing that really entertained the sullen teenager was the Turks' horrific use of terror tactics.

He eventually got out and, far from being grateful for his education, went to war with the Ottomans. Radu, who had stayed in Constantinople and converted to Islam, was appointed a commander of the army. His mission, which he chose to accept, was to destroy Vlad and rule in his stead. The warring pair became known by the Turks as "the Blood Brothers."

FRENCH REVOLUTION

FRANCE, 1789

Whatever you do, don't lose your head!

You know those parties that people you don't know very well hold when their parents go on vacation? The ones that start out with a few friends and end up with the police being called?

A mob stormed the Bastile fortress in Paris and killed the governor.

The French Revolution started out sensibly enough....

Many people were sick and tired of the king and the Church telling them what to do. They were hungry, poor, and forced to pay more and more taxes—and they'd had enough. Some tried to create their own National Assembly so they could have a say in how the country was run. But the king closed the hall, so they moved to a nearby tennis court, taking an oath never to part until France had a constitution. So far so good. Then things got a bit out of hand.

Events moved fast, with citizens acting as a mob rather than thinking for themselves. Democratic people were trying to bring in serious changes like the Declaration of the Rights of Man at the same time that hordes of hungry folk were acting on their guts.

The mob who stormed the Bastille prison on a torrent of misinformation and rumors didn't have any tools, so they tore down the fortress by hand, stone by stone. There were only seven prisoners inside—four forgers, two "lunatics," and weirdo Marquis de Sade—but the tower was a symbol of the monarchy. The revolutionaries set upon the governor of the jail, stabbed him repeatedly, sawed off his head, and then stuck it on a pike and paraded it through the streets.

A mass of starving women marched on the palace at Versailles, screaming for bread. In the country, chateaux were attacked, and rumors led to *La Grande Peur*—The Great Fear.

On January 17, 1793, King Louis XVI was condemned to death. Four days later, "Citizen Capet" was executed by guillotine. Crowned heads of state around Europe were nervous about what was happening in France, and suddenly the country was not only fighting itself, but the rest of the continent as well. The mob was angry.

Riots, chaos, looting, and murder among neighbors were only overshadowed by the sheer number of people in line for the guillotine. In Nantes a series of *noyades*, or mass drownings, usually of priests but sometimes people whose only crime was not being enthusiastic enough about the revolution, gave the city its nickname "the national bathtub."

Officially, 16,594 people were tried and guillotined, but no one knows exactly how many more were executed without trial or died in prison. It could be as high as 40,000.

Charles Dickens said, "It was the best of times; it was the worst of times." We just call it "The Terror."

What Was All the Fuss About?

No one can agree exactly why the French people revolted against their king, their church, and even themselves near the end of the eighteenth century, but one thing's certain: it was going to happen sometime. The old order, the Ancien Régime, was creaking with injustice. The aristocracy lived in sumptuous splendor, all silks and satins, dining on fine foods and traveling in glamorous coaches. The bishops were nearly as extravagant. The "third estate"—that's everyone else—paid for it. Harvests were bad, there were taxes on everything, and after an expensive war, the country was nearly broke. The peasants were exhausted, yet the closest the nobles ever came to working was when Queen Marie Antoinette dressed up as a milkmaid to play on her miniature farm.

The aristocracy just didn't get what the poor were complaining about. Marie Antoinette never actually said, "Let them eat cake!" when she was told the peasants couldn't buy bread, but she probably thought it!

Marie Antoinette

It's safe to say Marie Antoinette was never a princess of the people. From the moment she arrived to be Louis XVI's queen, "the Austrian Woman" became a symbol of everything extravagant and bad about the aristocracy. She wasn't always as excessive as people thought she was, but her expensive tastes did nothing to help her case later on. It didn't take much for the rumored story that she had defrauded a jeweler of a diamond necklace to become a major scandal.

The royal family decided to make a run for it, but they didn't have the hang of traveling in disguise. It's said the queen was wearing her strong, distinctive perfume, and the king poked his head out of the window of his not-hard-to-spot coach, forgetting his lifelike portrait was on every bank note in the land. Unsurprisingly, they were recognized and dragged back to Paris as prisoners.

However silly, pretty, or frivolous her subjects might once have seen her, by the time the queen, now called "Widow Capet," was executed, she was broken—stripped of her fine clothes, hair shorn off so as not to blunt the guillotine's blade, and trundled through the streets of Paris in an open cart, her hands tied. Her last words were an apology for treading on the executioner's foot.

High-Four

French courtiers used to show off how wealthy they were by wearing enormous wigs, or *perruques,* decorated with ribbons, bows, feathers, and jewels. They were powdered using poisonous white lead or even flour, which turned to glue in the rain, and they became so badly infested with lice they had to be boiled. Marie Antoinette's perruques could reach nearly four feet high. One of her wigs had an entire model battleship "sailing" through it.

What, No Pants?

French men could be divided into two types: those who wore "knickers" and those who didn't. The nobles wore satin pantaloons called "culottes" that were far too dainty for work, which was fine since nobles didn't do any work. The revolutionaries wore long trousers and called themselves "sans culottes"— "without knickers." They also wore floppy red *bonnets rouges,* or "Phrygian" caps, and rosettes, or "cockades" in the revolutionary colors: red, white, and blue.

A french noble and a revolutionary.

Wax Works

Anna Maria Grosholtz was the talented student of a medical wax-sculptor. She had already taken life masks from famous people such as Benjamin Franklin and the writer Voltaire, but now she was forced to turn her skills another way, clambering through piles of dead bodies looking for famous heads to immortalize. She cast a death mask from the decapitated king's head, and then she made the queen's likeness to add to her growing collection of celebrity wax works. She only narrowly escaped the guillotine herself and had a shaved head to prove it, but she was released so she could make a cast of the once-mighty Maximilien Robespierre's corpse. She later married a man named François Tussaud. Madame Tussaud's extraordinary collection still exists and is constantly expanding, though today's VIPs are usually sculpted after a live sitting.

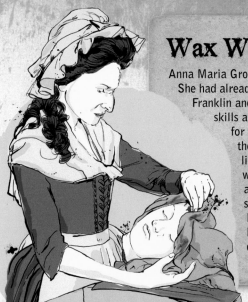

Madame Tussaud crafts a death mask.

Tricoteuses

Each day condemned prisoners would be dragged on an open wooden cart called a tumbrel to the Place de la Révolution (now the Place de la Concorde). It was a family day out. Parents brought their children, and everyone pushed and shoved for the best view. Street vendors even sold programs listing the people dying that day. Women called *tricoteuses* ("knitting women") sat at the foot of the scaffold, calmly knitting *bonnets rouges*. When the next victim was brought to the steps, they got up and started screaming, inciting the crowd to bay for their blood. Except when they didn't. Sometimes they just watched, without comment or expression, which was somehow even more disturbing.

Bals des Victimes

After the Reign of Terror, it was whispered *Bals des Victimes* ("Victims' Balls") were all the rage in secret, society salons. We don't know if these crazy dance parties held by the relatives of the dead actually happened or if they were just inventions made up to sell newspapers, but the idea stuck. Guests apparently would shave the back of their necks to imitate the way executioners sheared off the hair of their victims. Ladies wore thin red ribbons around their throats to look like they'd been slit, and instead of bowing to their partners, dancers would jerk their heads, pretending they were being cut off!

Madame Guillotine

In the old days, French executions involved strapping the victim onto a giant wheel, breaking all their bones with a club, and then rolling them around. The newfangled "guillotine" was based on execution machines called "The Scottish Maiden" and "The Halifax Gibbet," but their straight blades often got jammed because they crushed the victim's neck instead of cutting it. The problem was solved by making the blade triangular.

MASS FEAR IN OLD LONDON TOWN

Maybe it's the murky streets, foggy and forbidding, or maybe Londoners just love a good tale, but the city is full of terrifying bugaboos....

Mohocks

In 1712, a group of young thugs calling themselves Mohocks (after a delegation of Mohawk Indians who had visited Queen Anne) terrorized the streets of London.

After drinking up at local taverns, the young hooligans rampaged through alleyways stabbing, beating, and torturing anyone they met.

The ballad sheets and newspapers reported slit noses and stabbed cheeks. They described "tipping the lion," where someone's nose was pressed in and their eyes pressed out. "Dancing Masters" made people jump in the air by stabbing their legs. One gang rolled a terrified old woman down a hill inside a barrel.

On the few occasions one of these young men was caught, he would mysteriously be released without charge, which fueled rumors that Mohocks were high-ranking oafs with friends in very high places.

Even at the time, it was difficult to prove the Mohocks actually existed as an organized gang, but it's just one of many mobs that have plagued the city over the centuries.

The London Monster

Back in 1790, a monster stalked the streets. Ladies out walking would suddenly be stabbed in the thigh or the bottom. Sometimes a strange man would invite girls to sniff a bouquet of flowers that had a pin hidden inside, cutting their faces.

The newspapers went crazy, describing the attacks in lurid detail. People were scared to go out. Women started wearing metal petticoats; those who couldn't afford them tied saucepans under their skirts.

Monster Mania really took hold when £100 (about $142) was offered as a reward for the Monster's capture. People were accused left and right. Someone only had to point a finger for a mob to form out of nowhere and attack some poor guy for no reason.

It was said the Monster only attacked beautiful women, so some ladies claimed injury so everyone would know how gorgeous they were. One group of gentlemen even formed a "No Monster" club and wore badges to "prove" they weren't the monster!

An unfortunate artificial-flower maker was eventually imprisoned for the crime, despite iron-clad alibis and good character witness statements. He spent his imprisonment usefully, though, selling fake flowers to gentlefolk who'd come to stare at "The Monster."

Spring-Heeled Jack

He was a madman, a mass murderer, a ghost—perhaps even the Devil himself. He was as tall as a giant, with blazing red eyes, long talons, and springs on his boots so he could jump high over hedges and roofs. He spouted blue flame from his hideous mouth and carried away maidens in the dead of night. Everyone in 1830s London could describe Spring-Heeled Jack. However, there were very few actual sightings of him.

There were two reported cases where young girls described their attacker as having hideous claws and spewing flames, but even their evidence was very scanty, and other witnesses weren't so sure. This didn't stop the newspapers from picking up on the case with glee. The "Penny Dreadful" storybooks created wild tales about him, and soon Spring-Heeled Jack was everyone's favorite bad guy. Once again Londoners feared to leave their houses at night.

Dandy Highwaymen

Just outside London lay heathland. Its dark, bushy shadows were perfect hiding places for robbers on horseback. Newspapers couldn't decide whether highwaymen were romantic figures in lace cuffs, black capes, and tricorn hats who wielded pistols, bowed to ladies, and shouted "Stand and deliver!" or dangerous cutthroats every traveler must fear, so they painted them both ways.

Most highwaymen were not "gentlemen" of the road. They were just thugs, but one or two—such as Claude Duval, who reputedly danced with a lady he was robbing, or James Hind, who, as a Royalist, only attacked parliamentarians—were responsible for the legends that have sprung up around them. The most famous of all, Dick Turpin, must have been busy, as he supposedly haunted virtually every heath in London and drank at every tavern!

PIRATES

Avast! Shiver me timbers, me hearties, there be pirates out there on the seven seas!

The world has always had pirates. Ancient Greek, Phoenician, and Roman "gentlemen o' fortune" roamed the Mediterranean Sea, and for Vikings, looting and pillaging was all in a day's work.

In later centuries there was a very fine line between your all-out-bad-guy pirates and "legal" privateers. British sea dogs, such as Sir Francis Drake and Sir Walter Raleigh, were actively encouraged by Queen Elizabeth I to attack Spanish ships. Other privateers followed, covered by "letters of marque" issued by national governments allowing them to strike anyone who wasn't from their own country.

Eventually many privateers joined the true, illegal pirates, turning their beady eyes to merchant ships, which were heavy with costly cargo and light on cannons. The East India Company, trading in exotic spices, was a popular target.

By the 1630s, pirates were plaguing the Caribbean, but the Golden Age of Piracy of the seventeenth and eighteenth centuries saw buccaneers wherever there was water and potential booty. Some spectacular skulduggery took place around Madagascar.

The buccaneering world was brutal, but it was also one of the most democratic societies of the eighteenth century. A lot of ex-slaves joined up because every scurvy swab was treated equally on a pirate ship. There were even pirate codes, where everyone got a share of the plunder. You got compensation if your leg was shot off, and prizes were given to whoever first sighted a victim's sails, but punishments were hideous if you broke the rules. You could be marooned on a desert island, flogged, shot—or anything else your shipmates could think of! There's no evidence anyone ever had to walk the plank, but there was always the threat of being keelhauled—dragged right under the ship and up the other side on a very long rope. Of course the pirate code went out the porthole when the crew mutinied, which was often.

Life as a pirate was tough, but no tougher than that of a regular sailor. It was less regimented and promised better payoffs with all that lovely booty. The chances of promotion were excellent since few people, including the captain, lived very long. There were just so many ways to die at sea. You could be blown apart by cannonballs, slashed to death in hand-to-hand combat, blasted by one of the frequent storms, or fall overboard and be eaten by sharks.

If you were lucky, you might just lose an arm or a leg. Your limb would be sawed off by the ship's carpenter. You might use a hook or a peg leg—if you stopped bleeding long enough to live. If you lost an eye, you could always wear a patch like French corsair Olivier Levasseur, which would make you look extra mean. Edward "Blackbeard" Teach took his tough image even further, sticking fireworks into his beard so he looked like the devil!

The cleverest pirates lived on their reputations. They made sure that by the time the stories about them had been told in every tavern, embroidered with even more gory details at each telling, they only needed to shake their cutlasses or fire their pistols into the air and victims would hand over their cash without a murmur.

You didn't have to be a man to be a pirate. Some women dressed as men, but others didn't care and captained their ships in dresses. Ching Shih terrorized the South China Sea with a gigantic pirate armada. The Irish "Sea Queen of Connaught," Grace O'Malley, famously met Queen Elizabeth I of England (they got along rather well), but history's most famous female freebooters, Mary Read and Anne Bonny, preferred swashbuckling to schmoozing. Anne Bonny once dressed a dummy as a dead body, smothered it with fake blood, and then, just as a merchant ship passed by, raised her axe to "kill it." The terrified sailors surrendered immediately.

Anne Bonny used clever tactics to get sailors to surrender to her band of pirates.

The Flying Gang

In 1706, some of the most brazen ex-privateers formed the Pirates' Republic of Nassau on New Providence Island in the Bahamas. The two ringleaders, Benjamin Hornigold and Henry Jennings, hated each other, but they realized that by working together, they could create even more terror and get even more loot. Their "Flying Gang" included Blackbeard, Black Sam, and Calico Jack.

A Short Rope and a Long Drop

Bad luck to you if you got caught by the Royal Navy. Condemned pirates found themselves on the wrong end of "a short rope and a long drop."

Pirates' nooses were shorter than those of other criminals, which meant they didn't fall far enough for their necks to break. Instead, they were slowly strangled to death, their bodies twitching in what was known as the "Marshal's Dance." Their corpses were left dangling until three tides had washed over them.

The bodies of the "worst" pirates were gibbeted—hung in iron cages as warnings. Captain Kidd's rotting body was gibbeted over the River Thames for three years.

Samuel "Black Sam" Bellamy.

Pirate Weapons

The buccaneer's weapon of choice was his cutlass. A curved saber, it could slice through humans as effectively as the ropes, canvas, and wood on their ships. It also looked really cool, and since pirates traded on their image, it was an essential part of their pirate kit.

No scourge of the seas worth his doubloons would be caught dead without his firearm. Samuel "Black Sam" Bellamy carried four dueling pistols in his sash. They were usually flintlocks that, although deadly, were hard to load and often misfired.

Blackbeard's ship, the *Queen Anne's Revenge*, had no fewer than 40 cannons, but when its wreck was found, archaeologists discovered the crew didn't use many cannonballs. Instead, they fired anything nasty they could find, known as "langrage." Lead shot, nails, spikes, and broken glass were intended to kill the crew without damaging their valuable ship.

Treasure Maps

Captain William Kidd buried some of his booty on Gardiners Island in New York. It was discovered and used as evidence at his trial, but left a bigger mystery. A few days before his execution, Kidd wrote to the Speaker of the House of Commons, offering to reveal the rest of his treasure if his life was spared. The offer was refused, so we'll never know if he was telling the truth.

Olivier Levasseur one-upped him and pulled a parchment from around his neck seconds before his execution. He tossed it into the crowd, claiming anyone who could solve the 17-line puzzle written on it could find his buried stash!

Pieces of Eight

Silver coins known as "pieces of eight" were originally Spanish, but they were accepted all over the world, which meant everybody wanted them. Blackbeard stole so many that he had to weigh his!

Pirate treasure was often exactly that—silver, gold, diamonds, and jewels—but luxury goods were equally coveted by the highwaymen of the sea. Spices, silks, sugar, tobacco, cocoa, and alcohol were just some of the goodies on a pirate shopping list, but they'd steal boring, everyday items, too, if they needed them. Workmen's tools, medicines, frying pans, kettles, candles, and even soap found their way into a seasoned sea-rover's swag bag. And who said pirates were dirty?

Jolly Roger

Pirate flags were originally just red or black sheets (red for bloodshed, black for death), but most buccaneers added their own grisly touches. Some people claim the name comes from the French *Jolie Rouge* ("pretty red"); others say it's from "Old Roger," an ancient nickname for the devil.

Blackbeard's Jolly Roger was a skeleton piercing a heart with an arrow and raising a toast to Satan. Bartholomew "Black Bart" Roberts's flag showed him and the devil with an hourglass, telling the victim his time was up.

The pirate flag often depicted a skull and crossbones, but the one flown by John "Calico Jack" Rackham, a skull and crossed cutlasses, set the trend for the Jolly Roger we know today.

Most notorious pirate captains had their own flags.

Terror Tactics

While most pirates didn't want to deal with the trouble of torturing and killing their victims, some were just plain vicious.

French corsair Daniel Montbars was so cruel he was known as "The Exterminator." He once stabbed a victim in the stomach, pulled out his intestines, nailed them to a post, and then forced the unfortunate man to literally "dance" to death by hitting him on the backside with a burning log!

François L'Ollonais perfected a particularly grotesque form of torture. "Woolding" involved tying a rope around a prisoner's neck until his eyes popped out. L'Ollonais cut another man's still-beating heart out of his chest and started eating it in front of him!

After bloodthirsty buccaneer Edward Low cut off a Portuguese sea captain's lips, cooked them, and forced the man to eat them while they were still hot, even his crew was disgusted, calling Low a maniac and a brute.

Francis L'Ollonais "woolding" a victim.

François L'Ollonais

Jean-David Nau, aka François L'Ollonais, didn't buy the old adage "Dead men tell no tales." He liked dead men, especially dead Spaniards, but he always left one sailor alive to warn the rest.

Perhaps the most bloodthirsty of all buccaneers, L'Ollonais was driven by revenge after he was treated badly as a servant in the Caribbean when he was young. Early on in his buccaneering career, he was attacked by Spanish soldiers. He escaped by covering himself in blood and hiding under the bodies of his dead shipmates. He declared from then on he would never "give quarter to any Spaniard whatsoever."

He was as good as his word, slicing up his victims bit by bit, beheading entire crews, and killing indiscriminately, even when a ransom was paid. He often tortured for no purpose other than his own pleasure.

Fancy Dress

Velvet frock coats, powdered wigs, and tricorn hats were fashionable everywhere in the eighteenth century, but with all that lovely loot from their last raid jingling in their pockets, many pirate captains couldn't resist a bit of pirate bling.

Captain Kidd, Calico Jack, and Black Bart were all famous for their flashy fashions. Black Sam got his name from his flowing black hair, tied with a black satin ribbon, rather than because he was particularly evil—in fact, people were rather fond of him. He swaggered around in fancy breeches, silk stockings, and deep velvet cuffs, and had silver buckles on his shoes.

Regular shipmates—shinning up rigging, swabbing, and manning the crow's nest—wore much more practical items. "Slops" were simple canvas trousers, and headscarves kept the sun off their grizzled heads. Gold earrings were believed to guard against seasickness. Many regular sailors also wore earrings so that if they were shipwrecked and washed up dead on a foreign shore, they'd at least have enough gold to pay for their burial.

Fate caught up with him, though. Trying to escape from the Spanish in South America, he was captured by locals who cut him into pieces and cooked him. Some accounts go on to say that they ate him, too, but a villain as barbaric as L'Ollonais must have tasted pretty bad….

Blackbeard

Everyone knew the wild stories about Blackbeard the Pirate King. He had fourteen wives. His beard blazed with fire. He consorted with the devil. His ship was alive and would only obey the captain himself. In reality, Edward Teach was more audacious than violent, kidnapping rather than killing, stealing rather than torturing, and treating hostages honorably—for a pirate, that is. He had a sash full of pistols and cutlasses, but there's no evidence he actually took part in a swordfight until the very end.

The notorious buccaneer was finally tracked down by Lieutenant Robert Maynard of the Royal Navy as he held a party for some old pirate buddies from his Flying Gang days. The salty old sea dog was caught by surprise, but he put up a fight. Flintlocks were fired. Blades slashed. Blackbeard's cutlass broke Maynard's sword, but he was surrounded and died from multiple stab wounds.

Blackbeard's head was cut off and slung from Maynard's ship. The rest of his corpse was thrown overboard. Local legend says it swam around the ship three times before it died. His ghost is said to roam the waters still, searching for its missing head.

Edward Teach, more commonly known as "Blackbeard," was called the Pirate King.

CHICAGO DEATH HOTEL

USA, 1893

Traveling to the World's Fair? Why not stay at our beautiful new hotel? Here's why not....

The "murder hotel" in Chicago.

Herman Mudgett, aka Dr. H. H. Holmes, was one of America's first serial killers. He took advantage of the anonymity of cities, a burgeoning medical profession, and fast-moving technological innovations. Thankfully, in the end, technology would take advantage of him.

In the 1890s, Holmes built one of the world's scariest buildings: a "hotel" that was actually a murder machine. By hiring and firing different workmen for each part built, he ensured that he was the only guy who knew exactly how the labyrinth of corridors, chutes, doorways, dead ends, and windowless rooms worked. His employees, hotel guests, friends, girlfriends, business associates, and even his multiple wives never found out what went on up on the third floor and down in the basement—until it was too late.

Holmes enjoyed killing, but it wasn't just a hobby. As a medical student, he'd dissected hundreds of cadavers and become friendly with the hospital's crooked janitor

who acquired and sold bodies, no questions asked. Holmes realized he could kill people, cut them up, and sell not only their body parts but their bones as well. Universities were crying out for "articulated skeletons," and Holmes was already skilled at building, jointing, and polishing top-quality specimens. He could even supply to order. Need an extra tall skeleton or a small child? No problem.

Then he hit on the most brilliant thing of all: Why not get paid to kill people?

Holmes was very keen on the new concept of women in the workplace and even set up a ladies' employment agency for typists, housemaids, and shop assistants. Whenever he took on staff, he told them one of the "perks" of employment was life insurance. Holmes paid the premium, but he was also the beneficiary "should anything happen." It did. A lot.

Because of the World's Fair, a lot of people came to stay at the hotel. When they didn't come home, their families often just assumed they'd chosen to stay away. If anyone came looking for their family member, Holmes dispatched them too.

A connoisseur of killing, Holmes liked variety. His "castle," as he called it, was a chocolate box of murder methods—every one of them rotten.

Holmes could supply articulated skeletons to order for universities and hospitals.

H. H. Holmes

Herman Mudgett was an introverted child, building scarecrows and perpetual motion machines. He claimed other kids bullied him by locking him in a doctor's office with a skeleton. Instead of being scared of it, though, he was fascinated and became obsessed with death.

He started out stealing bodies for dissection but realized he could take out insurance policies on them and pocket the money. He also dealt in corrupt real estate, horse swindling, and other shady businesses.

Holmes wanted to fake his own death but couldn't find the right body, so he enticed his best friend to a hotel, where he

The Basement

Holmes's basement was a veritable chamber of horrors. He used it as his operating room. Bodies were sent down a chute where he stripped off the flesh in carbolic acid baths, dissected them for organs, and then created skeletons for medical schools, washing the bones in bleach to whiten them. It was a profitable business. A mounted, fully articulated skeleton fetched $170. Anything he had left over, he dissolved in lime pits or incinerated in a furnace.

dosed him with laudanum (opium). After dressing the corpse in his own clothes, he dumped it and, cool as a cucumber, collected the insurance money.

Holmes was arrested for a horse racket and briefly imprisoned before being bailed out. While inside, he started chatting with a convicted train robber, Marion Hedgepeth, aka "the Handsome Bandit." Holmes promised Hedgepeth $500 for the name of a shady lawyer. Hedgepeth supplied the name; Holmes didn't supply the cash. It was a debt he probably should have paid.

Chicago World's Fair

Held in 1893 at Jackson Park, Chicago, the World's Columbian Exposition officially celebrated the 400th anniversary of Christopher Columbus's landing in America.

The United States was enjoying a golden age. Business was booming, and people were getting rich. Chicago was still a bit of a backwater, but it was up and coming and desperate to host the fair. London had its Crystal Palace, Paris had the Eiffel Tower—and Chicago was to build the most magnificent of all, the White City.

It was a triumph. Designed by Daniel Burnham, who also built the Flatiron Building in New York City and Union Station in Washington, D.C., the park glowed with a million newfangled electric lights. Many people had never experienced electricity—but the fair was full of many other amazing new marvels. Moving pictures! Belly dancers! Camels! Zippers! Dishwashers! Shredded Wheat! Juicy Fruit chewing gum! Nothing like it had ever been seen before.

Twenty-eight million people visited the fair. Not all of them came home.

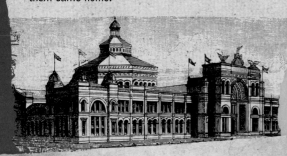

A belly dancer at the World's Fair.

Modus Operandi

Holmes couldn't murder anyone he was going to sell in a way that might damage the corpse. He soundproofed his rooms and fed gas lines into them to asphyxiate victims. He locked people in a bank vault and left them to suffocate, or simply poisoned them. If he wanted to kill guests as they slept, he preferred chloroform, but the druggist downstairs was getting suspicious about the amounts Holmes kept buying.

Other bodies he just needed to get rid of. He lined rooms with metal plates to conduct heat, and then he installed blowtorches and incinerated his victims. One room was a secret hanging chamber. It included a handy set of chutes leading down to the cellar.

The Castle

Holmes bought a drugstore a few blocks from Jackson Park via a couple of low-level scams. He immediately started building a three-story, block-long "castle."

The World's Fair Hotel opened in 1893. Its ground floor had a drugstore, jewelry business, and other glamorous shops, and the first level opened to fancy guest bedrooms and Holmes's offices. The whole place enjoyed newfangled gas lighting. Visitors didn't notice the other gas pipes leading to rooms the janitor was never allowed to clean.

The rest of the building housed a maze: rooms with no windows, doorways opening to brick walls, sinister "cupboards," weird-angled stairs, doors with no handles, and chambers with seemingly no entrance at all.

Family Matters

Police narrowly missed catching Holmes when they went to interview him about a minor fraud and failed to notice several boxes of body parts awaiting shipment, but Holmes was getting nervous. He'd killed so many people that there was a backlog of corpses.

Holmes moved to Fort Worth, Texas, where he had "inherited" property from two of his victims.

He had always dreamed of the ultimate insurance scam: an entire family. He persuaded his henchman, Benjamin Pitezel, to fake his own death and share the insurance payout with Holmes. Pitezel was to pose as a nutty scientist who accidentally "died" in a lab explosion. Holmes promised to find a body to "be" Pitezel, but instead just murdered his friend.

He told Mrs. Pitezel her husband was in London and persuaded her to give him custody of her three youngest children....

The Net Closes

Forensic science had progressed far enough to prove the chloroform Benjamin Pitezel had "committed suicide" with had actually been administered after his death.

A Toronto cellar revealed two small bodies that turned out to be Alice and Nellie Pitezel. Detective Frank Geyer of the Pinkerton Agency deciphered letters that led to eight-year-old Howard Pitezel's remains, stuffed up in a chimney in Indianapolis.

Meanwhile, Holmes's former cellmate, Marion Hedgepeth, was still angry at not getting his $500. He spilled the beans, and Holmes was arrested, held on horse theft charges because they had no evidence—yet.

It took a month to investigate the Castle's labyrinth of torture chambers. Police found human skeletons, a dissection table covered with blood, and a pile of bloody clothes. A giant ball of hair was decaying under the stairs, and deep lime pits overflowed with decomposing bones.

Marion Hedgepeth tells the police everything he knows aboabout H. H. Holmes' crimes.

Celebrity Criminal

Holmes turned into a showman. While in prison he wrote a book and became a minor "celebrity" as an insurance fraudster. When bodies were discovered, though, things changed.

The newspapers had a field day as more and more crimes surfaced. At the trial, Holmes changed his story on a regular basis.

It's hard to know exactly how many people he killed. He admitted to thirty, but three of the people he claimed he'd killed were actually still alive. There are twenty-seven "definites," but the jumble of bones and body parts at the castle could indicate as many as 200 victims. Holmes was hanged in 1896. His last request was to be buried in ten feet of cement, as he feared dissection!

The World's Fair Hotel was finally demolished in 1938. The site is currently a US Post Office.

EMPRESS WU ZETIAN

If you're going to be the only female emperor in 4,000 years, you'll need to be tough. Oh, and it helps not to be too devoted to your family....

CHINA, 624–705

Nearly 1,400 years after the "crime," it's hard to know if Consort Wu really murdered her own newborn daughter just so she could accuse her rival, Empress Wang, of the dirty deed. Traditional historians certainly thought she did, but it's also possible that Wang did it all along or that it could have just been a tragic case of sudden infant death syndrome. Whoever—or whatever—killed the baby, the result was the same: Wang was deposed and Wu eased nicely into the lead position as favorite of Emperor Gaozong.

Empress Wu Zetian.

Gaozong was twenty-one, weak and inexperienced. Wu was neither. She gave him advice on how to rule, and her power grew. Things were going well for the ambitious young concubine, but there was one problem. Empress Wang might have been deposed, but she was still around, which meant that Wu couldn't marry the emperor and that her sons couldn't inherit.

No, let's make that two problems. Second-favorite Consort Xiao was even more of a threat—she had a son who had been born before Wu's children.

There were no two ways about it for Wu: they all had to go.

Wu accused the two women of witchcraft and had them executed. Xiao's son was exiled, and officials who'd supported the former queen disappeared. The newly married Empress Wu, however, was only just beginning. She started getting rid of the rest of her enemies one by one. Some were exiled, some executed; some were even forced to commit suicide. A potential romantic rival was poisoned, and the blame was shifted onto two more of Wu's enemies. The result: three dead bodies for the price of one!

After the emperor became ill during a feast (there were whispers of slow poisoning, but his symptoms sound more like high blood pressure), he got even weaker. By now Wu was making all the decisions, standing behind a curtain and telling him what to say.

Wu's oldest sons, however, were showing signs of thinking for themselves. The oldest died in yet more suspicious circumstances.

Empress Wu, telling the Emperor what to say and what to do.

The second was accused of treason and demoted to the rank of commoner.

The emperor was in very poor health, but a few brave viziers opposed Wu becoming China's official regent. The luckiest were demoted. The rest were exiled or discovered dead in their chambers.

When Gaozong finally died, Wu's third son, Zhongzong, was sitting on the throne before the emperor was cold in his coffin. Wu was horrified to discover Zhongzong's wife was almost as scheming as Wu was. Zhongzong lasted barely six weeks before Wu replaced him with his younger brother Ruizong, who was much more easily manipulated. Ruizong was kept a virtual prisoner and never appeared in public.

Wu, now monarch in all but name, didn't even bother with a curtain anymore. No one was surprised when Ruizong "abdicated." After officially refusing the throne three times (a Chinese custom, not any shyness on Wu's part!), Wu Zetian humbly accepted the throne as the only woman ever to wear the yellow robe of emperor.

Wu Zetian

It is said when Wu Zetian was born, there was a total eclipse of the sun.

An extraordinarily bright child, well-read and educated (unusual for girls of the time), the young Wu was made a royal concubine at the age of thirteen. There were twenty-eight other consorts ahead of Wu, but she managed to attract the old Emperor Taizong's attention and became a sort of secretary to him, allowing her to continue her studies.

When emperors died, concubines usually had their heads shaved and were locked in a nunnery, but on Taizong's death, Wu had a lucky break. Wang, the wife of the new Emperor Gaozong, helped her escape because she thought Wu might help detract Gaozong's attention from her rival, Consort Xiao.

Poor Wang didn't know what she'd gotten herself into. Gaozong dropped Xiao—and Wu became his favorite instead. . . .

Wu had nightmares about herself as a mouse, with cats chasing her.

Human Pig

Traditional historians claim Wu ordered hideous deaths for her rivals Empress Wang and Consort Xiao. Their hands and feet were hacked off, and what was left of them was tossed into a vat of wine. A few days later, their bodies were taken out and beheaded.

This sounds suspiciously similar to a much earlier story about another ruthless empress from several hundred years ago, Lu Zhi of the Han Dynasty, who allegedly murdered a rival by gouging out her eyes, cutting off her arms and legs, and forcing her to drink acid before tossing the blind, limbless mute into the palace cesspit with the swine.

Whatever the method, both Wang and Xiao ended up dead.

Scary Empress, Decent Emperor

It would be easy to accuse Wu Zetian of being purely evil, but even her enemies had to admit she was a capable ruler. She was popular with ordinary Chinese folk, improving their living standards and bringing prosperity to the country. She avoided major wars and encouraged foreign ambassadors to visit from as far away as the Byzantine Empire in the west.

Wu introduced entrance exams for would-be bureaucrats, so people got jobs because they were good rather than because they were someone's relative. Of course, she didn't stand for any nonsense. Anyone seen as incompetent was instantly executed. The faintest whiff of rebellion from anyone, especially family, was crushed without mercy.

Nightmares

Empress Wang, it is said, took the news of her forthcoming execution quite well, merely commending herself to the emperor and new empress.

Xiao was having none of that. She was furious and cursed Wu, screaming to the heavens that she be reincarnated as a cat and Wu as a mouse so she could chase the monster and grab her by the throat. When the superstitious Wu heard about the curse, legend says she banned cats from the palace and from anywhere she visited, but it didn't work. She kept having nightmares about cats and about Wang and Xiao pursuing her with wild hair and bleeding stumps where the hands and feet should be.

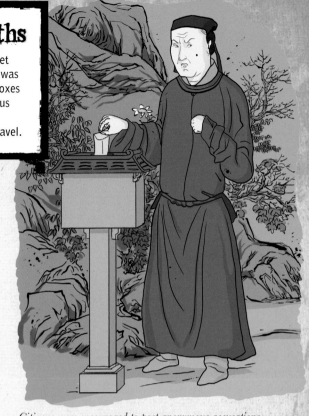

Fishy Findings

Wu needed to make sure everyone knew she had the right to reign. Just as she was manipulating herself to power, a mysterious stone oracle was pulled out of the Lô River. Its "ancient" carvings told how a Sage Mother would come to rule mankind, bringing eternal prosperity. Wu was delighted and, adding "Divine Mother" to her growing list of titles, rewarded her nephew, who had conveniently made the miraculous discovery, by making him prime minister.

Citizens were encouraged to post anonymous accusations into the Empress's mailboxes.

Next, an obliging monk unearthed a text called *The Great Cloud Sutra*, which predicted that the coming reincarnation of the Buddha Maitreya, or Buddha of the Future, would be as a female monarch. The world would be free of illness, worry, and disaster.

Wu immediately made sure there was a "Great Cloud" temple in every town and commissioned a massive statue of the Buddha Maitreya at the Longmen Caves. Many commented on its uncanny resemblance to—could it be?—no, surely not! Didn't it look just like the Empress Wu?

Nothing to Say

In the province of Shaanxi lies a mile-long "Spirit Road" lined with fabulous stone statues. It leads between two hills to the vast Qianling Mausoleum housing the mortal remains of Emperor Gaozong and Empress Wu. No one knows exactly what's inside the underground tomb, as it's never been looted by robbers nor excavated by archaeologists, but many believe its treasures would rival First Emperor Qin Shihuang's terra-cotta army.

A curious stone memorial to Empress Wu sits along the Spirit Road. Ornately decorated at the top, the place where long lists of an emperor's achievements would normally be carved has been left completely blank.

AL CAPONE

Grab your fedora hat, hide your tommy gun in a violin case, and catch the night train to Chicago, 1927. If you know the password, they might just let you in....

USA, 1920s

If you were down and out, starving after the 1929 Wall Street crash, you'd probably really like Al Capone. He'd just opened a free soup kitchen to help people exactly like you. You'd remember how he paid the hospital bill of an innocent passerby wounded by a bullet meant for him, and chuckle at how the jolly gangland boss rented fifty rooms at the Hotel Metropole and bought an entire Pullman railway car just so he could travel in peace and quiet. He was a regular Robin Hood, or so he liked people to think.

In truth the "folk hero" was a dangerous mobster who thought nothing of having friends, rivals—and anyone else who got in his way—disposed of. He owned speakeasy bars, dog tracks, casinos, and nightclubs, but his main caper was bootlegging—a very profitable business in Prohibition-era Chicago. His bars openly served illegal whisky, beer, and wine. His casinos staked thousands of dollars on each spin of the wheel. He pocketed hundreds of thousands of those dollars a month, though exactly how much we'll never know. Al Capone didn't have a bank account.

There was a darker side, too. Capone's thugs blew up joints that wouldn't serve his booze. His hoods bribed, intimidated, tortured, and murdered people. Juries were tampered with and murderers let off when witnesses suddenly retracted their statements.

The police considered the mobsters' violent attacks on each other to be a "private war" and left them to it.

Capone might have been the biggest boss in town, but he wasn't the only boss. Rivals were forever snapping at his heels, and he'd snap back. Mobsters hijacked each other's liquor vans, blew up each other's gin joints, and whacked each other's hitmen. Shootouts between gangs were legendary. The police considered it a private war, and as long as no officers got murdered, they left the criminals to kill each other.

Scarface

Al Capone had two nicknames. He liked it when his friends called him "Snorky"—slang for someone who dresses smartly in the latest fashions. He was less happy about what everyone else called him: "Scarface." Guess which name stuck?

He hated his three scars, red and angry, which seared across his cheek and neck. He tried to hide them with powder and always made photographers take pictures from his other side. If anyone asked, Capone said they were war wounds. He actually got them when he insulted a girl in a nightclub and her angry brother slashed his face with a knife.

The undertakers did very nicely, cooking up more ostentatious funeral processions behind which all manner of corrupt city officials, congressmen, district attorneys, and even the mayor himself would parade mournfully. After all, it had been the villains who secured their positions in the first place.

Al Capone always insisted he was just a businessman. "I make my money by supplying a public demand," he used to say. "Whatever else they may say, my booze has been good and my games have been on the square."

Al Capone

Alphonse Capone made his name in Chicago, but he was born in Brooklyn, New York. He was expelled from school for hitting a teacher in the face, though he always claimed she hit him first.

While older brother Vincenzo ran away to the west (he became a prohibition agent known as Richard "Two-Gun" Hart, wearing a tin sheriff's star and a giant Stetson hat), young Al fell in with the local street toughs.

He ended up with the Five Points Gang, where he became a bouncer, bodyguard, and muscle for his mentor, Johnny "The Fox" Torrio.

They moved to Chicago in 1920 to help out "Big" Jim Colosimo, aka "Diamond Jim," who was having some trouble with an extortion racket called the Black Hand. Colosimo had a big gambling, nightclub, and escort empire, but he didn't want to go into bootlegging.

Capone and Torrio disagreed. Colosimo was found mysteriously murdered. The culprit was never caught, but Torrio and Capone slid into front position. When Torrio retired, he handed control to the twenty-six-year-old Capone with the words: "Al, it's all yours."

Torrio meant the racket. Al took Chicago.

Prohibition

America always had its hard drinkers, even before the crazy, gun-slinging days of the Wild West. Civil War soldiers snuck bottles of booze into camp under their pants, earning the name "bootleggers."

Many fine, upstanding gentlefolk believed alcohol was the root of all the crime and violence in the country. They called for it to be banned altogether.

In 1920, they got their way. All production, imports, sales, and transport of alcohol were outlawed, but if the campaigners had dreamed of quiet family nights by the fireside sipping tea and reading the Bible, they had another thing coming.

Prohibition opened up a massive black market in smuggled alcohol, "speakeasy" nightclubs, and criminal activity. A new breed of racketeer began importing and even manufacturing illegal hooch. At first it was clandestine; they pretended the alcohol was for medical use. As the years went by, though, they became more brazen. Al Capone took bootlegging to a whole new level—he didn't even try to hide his breweries, as oddly, Chicago's city officials had no sense of curiosity . . . or, indeed, smell.

Tommy Guns

General John T. Thompson spent most of World War I developing a new type of submachine gun that could fire 1,000 rounds a minute and cut through steel plate. It took so long to perfect, though, that the war was over and the army didn't want it.

The police didn't want it either. The "tommy gun" was so jumpy it was impossible to hit anything accurately. All you could hope to do was press the trigger and spray a bunch of bullets in the general direction of your target. You could—and probably would—injure innocent bystanders.

In an ironic move, the "Chicago Typewriter" went on public sale instead in the Windy City's gun suppliers, hardware shops, and even drugstores. Now every bandit in town could buy a "Thompson Anti-Bandit Gun" of their very own. The violin case was extra....

Any mobster in town could buy a "Tommy Gun."

Twisted Turnout

In the 1920s, Chicago elections weren't just rigged—they were loaded.

Voters were intimidated, coerced, forced to vote at gunpoint, and occasionally bombed. Polling-day gunfights were normal. "Chain voting" was when someone entered the booth with a premarked ballot paper and brought out a fresh one for the hoods to mark for the next voter.

Capone didn't even bother rigging the 1924 Cicero election. He simply had the opposition voters hijacked, driven out of town, and left to walk back after the ballots closed. In 1927, more people appeared to have voted than there were actual electors!

The primary election campaign of 1928, in which the corrupt mayor of Chicago ran for president, saw sixty-two bombings. It became known as the "Pineapple Primary," as "pineapple" was the slang word for hand grenades!

Bloody Valentine

George "Bugs" Moran of the rival North Side Gang wanted revenge on Capone for killing his boss. He'd already tommy-gunned Capone's car and tried to whack him while he was eating lunch at the Hawthorne Inn. Now Capone had gone to live in Miami. While the cat was away, Moran thought he'd play. He'd take over Chicago….

On February 14, 1929, a bunch of "policemen" "raided" the garage where Bugs was to meet his gang. They lined the hoodlums along the wall, then opened fire.

When the real police turned up looking for their stolen car, they found seven bodies lying in a pool of blood. Bugs, who had arrived late, told them, "Only Capone kills like that."

Capone swore he was in Miami, and no charges were brought. But the public was getting fed up with all the violence. The tide was turning.

"Policemen" lining a rival gang up against the wall.

The Untouchables

Al Capone was an embarrassment to the government. The mobster had both police and local authorities in his pocket; there was no way to get to him.

Eliot Ness—who was a Prohibition agent, not a policeman—put together a team of men unlikely to succumb to blackmail or intimidation and declared a very public war on the gang lord.

Ness made sure the newspaper reporters were there whenever he staged a raid on a distillery or speakeasy, and when one of his men was approached with a bribe, he announced they were "incorruptible." The papers loved it.

In the end it wasn't Ness who broke Capone. Frank Wilson of the Internal Revenue Service (IRS) charged him with tax evasion, but it was Ness's team, "The Untouchables," that fired people's imagination. Perhaps good could overcome evil after all.

Behind Bars

Al Capone was sent to prison for eleven years, convicted for tax evasion, though he was suspected to have been involved in at least thirty murders and countless other crimes.

At first, prison life was pretty cushy. He had a comfy bed, plenty of alcohol, special meals delivered to his cell, and was even served Thanksgiving dinner by a butler. When he had guests, he used the prison governor's office.

Then the infamous Alcatraz Federal Penitentiary opened. On an island in San Francisco Bay, the prison was harsh, and the governor wasn't interested in bribes. Capone was one of the first inmates. By the time he was finally released, he was ravaged by disease. He never recovered.

DEATHS OF THE ROMAN EMPERORS

It was a dangerous job, Roman Emperor. In the early days, you might die of natural causes, though sometimes even that was suspicious. A slave could test everything you ate, and you might still get "food poisoning."

By the time the Roman Empire started to crumble, you were lucky if you lasted three months without being assassinated. Even if you weren't actually killed, you might be deposed, tortured, blinded, or have parts of you hacked off by your own men. Being forced to step down and go into exile was a mercy.

One of the most infamous assassinations is Julius Caesar, stabbed in the back by his own senators. But what was to come made his death almost boring. . . .

Thinking of applying for the vacancy "Emperor of All Ancient Rome"? Check the fine print. . . .

Caligula

As a child, Gaius liked to dress up in miniature armor and hang out with his dad's soldiers. They called him "Little Boots," after his military sandals. He might have been cute as a kid, but as emperor, "Caligula" became crazed with power.

He killed his cousin and had his grandmother poisoned. He then declared himself a god and put up statues so people could worship him. He hated his boyhood nickname, but he was called much worse. He had a very hairy body and no sense of humor. Anyone who even mentioned goats around him was put to death!

He burned people alive or flung them into the mines or circuses, declaring he wished the people of Rome had one neck so he could strangle them all at once.

Eventually even his own guards had enough of him. He was hacked to death, stabbed more than thirty times.

Commodus

If it was possible, Commodus was even crazier than Caligula—more interested in chariot racing than looking after his country. He had former friends killed; sometimes for their money, sometimes just because he didn't like them anymore. He fancied himself a gladiator, killing up to one hundred bears at a time. He once decapitated an ostrich and waved its head at his senators, implying he'd do the same to them. Things got so bad no one noticed when 2,000 people died of the plague in a single day. Everyone was too busy hiding from Commodus!

Despite numerous plots, Commodus proved difficult to get rid of. Finally, during Saturnalia (a big festival), he was taking a bath when his mistress, who'd just found out she was next on his death list, slipped some poison into his bedtime drink. Commodus was so drunk, however, he merely vomited it up, so a young athlete, Narcissus, was brought in to strangle him.

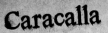

Caracalla

Bassanius, better known as Caracalla because of the hooded cloak he always wore, didn't start out well, murdering his own brother so he could become emperor. He did the usual bad-king stuff—building lavish palaces and hiking up taxes. He was obsessed with blood and forced his senators to provide him with exotic animals to kill. He executed a charioteer for being on the opposing team, and he declared himself a reincarnation of Alexander the Great.

Few people mourned when Caracalla was stabbed by a member of his personal bodyguard as he was relieving himself by the side of the road.

Elagabalus

At first the Roman people were rather taken by Elagabalus's good looks—until he decided everyone was going to worship the sun god Heliogabalus. He also had expensive tastes. He swam in perfumed pools, drove chariots drawn by elephants and lions, and never wore the same shoes twice. He sold top jobs to the highest bidder, went through several wives, and from the start, killed people willy-nilly.

He set his sights on murdering a nice young man, Alexanius. The army, sick and tired of Elagabalus's murderous tastes, rescued Alexanius, and then dragged out the emperor, who was hiding inside a chest. Elagabalus and his mother were decapitated, and their bodies were dragged around the streets. As a final insult, they were thrown into the River Tiber.

Valerian

As emperors go, Valerian could have been halfway decent (if you overlook the whole Christians-lions-persecution business....). Rome was in deep trouble, though. Previous bad rule had left the empire in shreds, and Valerian had to ride to Persia to fight King Shapur.

Valerian was captured and thrown into prison. There are various accounts of how he died, none of them nice. Some say he simply died a broken man; that would be his best hope. One ancient historian tells how Shapur used the emperor as a human footstool for mounting his horse. Another says Valerian was forced to drink molten gold. A third account has him skinned alive, stuffed with straw, and displayed in the temple.

VIKINGS

With 300 years of pillage and plunder under their tooled leather belts, the Vikings still rank as some of the bloodthirstiest bad guys in history.

In Old Norse, to "go on a viking" was to go raiding. Every young Northman dreamed of seeking fame and fortune by joining voyages of exploration and proving they were worthy of glory and respect. If the locals along the way weren't too keen on trading, or if they had some nice, shiny gold stuff, well, it would be rude not to pillage a bit....

Scandinavian seafarers traveled north to the arctic lands, and south to France, Spain, and Africa. Their longships sailed west to the British Isles and North America, and east into Russia and even Constantinople, now Istanbul in Turkey. They discovered whole regions and opened up trade routes. "Business partners," however, soon discovered the line between "trade" and "theft" for your average Viking was very fine. Sometimes it didn't exist at all.

Europe had become prosperous in the days since the Romans. Ports were wealthy and badly defended. They weren't

Vikings go on a raid.

prepared for sudden, vicious attacks by bearded barbarians whose aim was simple: steal as much plunder as possible, seize anyone who could be ransomed or sold as a slave, and kill everyone else. If they got a good battle in the bargain, even better.

The marauders spared no one. King Edmund of East Anglia was captured, used for archery practice, and beheaded. The peaceful monks of Lindisfarne in Northumberland were either massacred or dragged naked back to the raiders' ships to be sold as slaves. Poor old Alfege, the Archbishop of Canterbury, was "boned to death" by feasting Vikings chucking their leftovers at him.

The Archbishop of Canterbury was "boned to death" by feasting Vikings.

What shocked the Christian world was the Norsemen's disregard for churches and holy relics. It wasn't so much that the Vikings hated Christianity—they eventually converted themselves—more that they had their own, pagan gods. They just didn't care about the same things.

Not all folk from Scandinavia between 800 CE and 1100 CE were Vikings. Farmers, miners, craftsmen, and traders dwelt relatively peacefully in the inhospitable northlands of modern-day Norway, Denmark, and Sweden. They had their own alphabet (called runes), loved ale and mead, played board and dice games, dyed their hair, shaved, plucked their eyebrows, combed their hair, and even cleaned out their ears. The English were shocked to know they bathed—sometimes up to once a week!

As the North folk became richer and richer from all of that loot, though, many turned a greedy eye to foreign lands not as cold and unforgiving as their own. Early quick-and-dirty raids turned to all-out invasion.

The Norse stories and way of life survive through accounts such as the *Anglo-Saxon Chronicle* and their own sagas. Many of the tales were told around firesides for many years before being written down, and it can be hard to tell how much is fact and how much is a flight of the storyteller's fancy. The tales are so vivid, though, that it's easy to get a flavor for a brutal, violent, exciting world that talks of dragons and giants in the same breath as real battles and heroic deeds.

Viking sagas have become part of our own world folklore. We even still mention Norse gods every day of the week: Monday is Moon Day; Tuesday, Tyr's Day, for the god of the sky. Wednesday is Odin's or Wodan's Day; Thursday, Thor's Day; and Friday belongs to Freya, goddess of beauty.

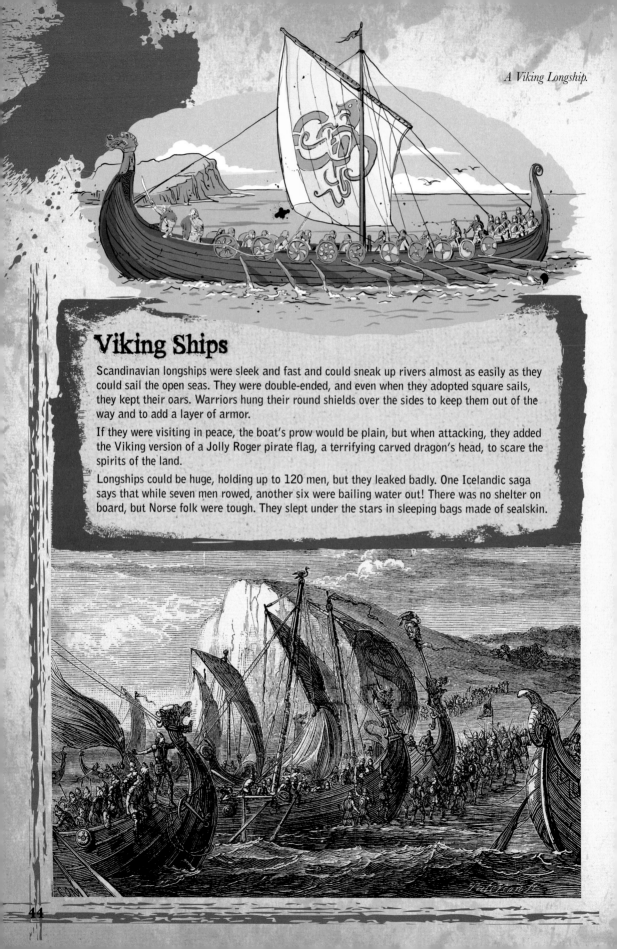

Viking Ships

Scandinavian longships were sleek and fast and could sneak up rivers almost as easily as they could sail the open seas. They were double-ended, and even when they adopted square sails, they kept their oars. Warriors hung their round shields over the sides to keep them out of the way and to add a layer of armor.

If they were visiting in peace, the boat's prow would be plain, but when attacking, they added the Viking version of a Jolly Roger pirate flag, a terrifying carved dragon's head, to scare the spirits of the land.

Longships could be huge, holding up to 120 men, but they leaked badly. One Icelandic saga says that while seven men rowed, another six were bailing water out! There was no shelter on board, but Norse folk were tough. They slept under the stars in sleeping bags made of sealskin.

Funerals

You really didn't want to be a slave at a Viking funeral, especially if it was for someone important. You'd be expected to "volunteer" to be sacrificed with them, so they could treat you badly in the afterlife, too!

One chronicle tells of a particularly freaky funeral. The dead chieftain was ceremonially dressed in his best clothes, laid in his longship, and given mead, food, and flowers to take with him to Valhalla. The lord's animals—his dogs, horses, and cows—were sliced in half and put in the boat with him.

Then came the slave girl's turn. She was led off into a tent by an old woman called the Angel of Death, and the men beat their shields really loudly to cover her screams as she was stabbed and strangled. She was put in the boat too, and the whole lot was set on fire.

Most Norse funerals weren't like that, of course—if all ships had been burned, we wouldn't have found so many buried with all their treasures.

Blood Eagle

The sagas tell of a horrific ordeal where the victim's rib cage was cut away from his spine and folded back like the wings of an eagle. His lungs were then dragged out and pinned back as a sacrifice to Odin. According to legend, the Northumbrian king Ællea was subjected to the Blood Eagle in revenge for his alleged murder of the fantastically named Ragnar Hairy Breeches.

Viking craftsmen created all kinds of things out of precious metals.

Treasure

Vikings loved treasure, and they had a lot of it. Some was lawfully gained by trading, but most of it was pillaged or extorted from terrified local kings who tried to buy them off with bribes. It didn't work. Having extracted one batch of "Danegeld" (Dane-gold), the raiders just came back for more. Archaeologists have found coins and treasure from all over the ancient world at Viking burial sites.

Scandinavian folk created treasures of their own, though. They had skilled craftsmen who worked in precious metals, creating jewelry, sword hilts, and other decorative objects.

Because they were usually traveling, warriors liked to carry their wealth with them. They clasped their cloaks with fabulous brooches and wore fancy buckles on their belts, usually bronze but sometimes gold or silver. Some wore "hacksilver," jewelry that could be chopped up and used as money on the road.

Berserkers

Berserkers were the fellows other Vikings thought went a bit too far. Bear-Shirts and Wolf-Coats wore animal skins and acted like mad dogs, strong as bears or bulls.

These guys worked themselves up into frenzied madness, some say with poisonous mushrooms and honey wine, known as mead. They became so crazy that they didn't feel pain as they tore into battle, bellowing and shrieking, axes flailing, killing right and left. The chronicles say neither fire nor iron affected them. Just the sight of these nutcases was enough to make an enemy turn and run.

Considered dangerous bullies who'd pick a fight over nothing, they were nevertheless very useful in a brawl. Berserkers may be the source for terrified travelers' tales of Vikings shape-shifting themselves into bears, wolves, and trolls.

Viking berserkers wore animal skins and acted like mad dogs.

Gods

Vikings believed the world was made up of three flat discs on top of each other, with a giant ash tree called Yggdrasil growing through the middle. Underneath, the dragon Nidhogg gnawed at Yggdrasil's roots. A squirrel called Ratatoskr ran up and down the tree carrying rude messages from Nidhogg to a stately eagle that lived in the branches at the top.

The Norse gods lived in Asgard on the top level, ruled by Odin from his palace, Valhalla. Odin traded one of his eyes for his legendary wisdom. He was kept up to date with world news by his two ravens, Thought and Memory.

Thor was the god of Thunder and carried a great hammer that could smash mountains. Popular with warriors because of his bravery, Thor loved a good skirmish, but wasn't very bright. He was always being called out by the trickster god Loki, who was cunning, vindictive, and inventive, but could, very occasionally, be a good guy. Loki could change shape at will and was definitely not to be trusted.

Humans lived across the rainbow bridge Bifröst in Midgard, which they shared with giants, dwarves, and elves.

The Norse underworld, Niflheim, was a terrifying realm of frozen rivers, ruled by the horrific goddess Hel. That's where you ended up if you lived a boring life or didn't die heroically—a good reminder to men going into battle to fight hard and die well.

Weapons

All free Norsemen had to own weapons. There was nothing a Viking liked better than getting up close and dirty with his enemy, so hand-to-hand "melee" weapons associated with Thor and Odin were their favorites.

Swords were forged using twisted metal for super strength and tested by floating a human hair down the edge. Most were double-edged and had rounded ends, but don't be fooled. These blades were nasty, designed to slash rather than stab. To add mystery, they had names, such as Leg Biter, War Snake, Widow Maker, Odin's Flame, Torch of the Blood, and Battle-Flasher.

Vikings also loved axes. You needed muscles to wield one properly, though, as well as pinpoint accuracy. If you missed, you'd swing around like an idiot, stab yourself in the back, or even end up with it stuck in the ground, leaving you vulnerable (and everyone else laughing) while you tried to pull it out.

Some helmets were metal, but none had horns on them; they would have gotten in the way of all that axe-swinging.

Harald Hardrada's chainmail shirt was so tough it was said nothing could pierce it, but it was also so long it looked like a dress. His men nicknamed it "Emma." Sadly, Harald left Emma on board his ship when he went to fight King Harold of England in 1066—and was killed.

Valhalla

Big Daddy of the Gods, Odin, dwelled in a palace called Valhalla. Its walls were made of spears and its roof of interlocked shields. Every day dead warriors fought each other in bloody but friendly combat; every night they magically returned to life and feasted 'til dawn.

The last thing a Norse warrior wanted was to die peacefully tucked in bed. He knew the only way to get to Valhalla was to die gloriously in battle. Only the truly valiant would be chosen by the Valkyries, petrifying winged warrior-maidens, to live in the Hall of the Slain.

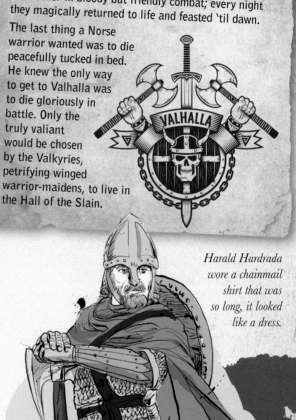

Harald Hardrada wore a chainmail shirt that was so long, it looked like a dress.

RICHARD III
ENGLAND, 1485

England's most fascinating murder mystery, still unsolved for over 500 years.

The battlefield is hot, filthy, and drenched with gore. All around you soldiers clash, hacking limbs and stabbing guts. Blood spurts through metal as the eye slits of helmets are pierced with terrifying accuracy. That's one thing you don't have to worry about— you lost your own helmet some time ago. They know who you are, though; they're coming to get you. There's only one thing left. Fight, and to the death....

The Battle of Bosworth saw the end of medieval England and the beginning of "modern times." King Richard III had reigned for two years, two months, and one day, but that was about to end. He went down fighting—the last English monarch to die in battle. His challenger, Henry Tudor, was crowned then and there

before sneakily backdating his accession so he could call anyone who'd fought for the defeated king a traitor. Of course, the worst traitor of all, or at least according to Henry, was Richard himself.

Richard, Duke of Gloucester, started out as a decent guy. When his brother Edward IV died, Richard was named Lord Protector of twelve-year-old Edward V.

King Richard III was the last English king to die in battle.

Everyone, including the boy's nine-year-old brother, traveled to the Tower of London, and preparations began for the coronation. Before the young king could be crowned, however, he was "proved" to be illegitimate, as his parents' marriage was declared invalid.

Uncle Richard was put on the throne instead. No one saw either of the two princes again.

The stories started almost immediately after Richard's death. According to John Rous, a very unreliable historian, Richard was born after his mother had been pregnant for two years. He'd had hair down to his shoulders and a full set of teeth! Rous claimed Richard was responsible for the death of a previous king, Henry VI, and Richard's own wife, Anne. Since Rous had actually written a previous "history" praising Richard to the heavens a few years earlier, his writing needs to be taken with a very large grain of salt. Thomas More called Richard "hard favored," and other historians waded in, too. Richard's "crimes" mounted up, and the public loved it. Over the years, the rumors became "truth."

Henry VII

As a minor member of one of the warring families, Henry Tudor wasn't an obvious choice for king, but these were unstable times. Disease, battle, assassination, murder, and execution were all in a day's work for a contender to the throne. Possible challengers came and went until twenty-eight-year-old Henry found himself the front-runner and rather liked the idea.

He'd been in exile in France and knew that if he wanted the crown, he'd have to strike fast, before King Richard had a chance to muster reinforcements.

Richard III ruled for only two years, two months, and one day.

Richard III

One of the greatest murder mysteries of all time is the legend of Richard III, a man notorious as a "killer." Does he deserve his reputation as a black-hearted villain? Many argue probably not.

Is he completely innocent, then? Many also argue probably not, but that doesn't necessarily make him any worse than others of the time. Quietly disposing of a couple of inconvenient children to get your hands on the crown would have been seen as unpleasant but necessary by more than one challenger through the ages.

Given we have very little evidence at all, we have no reason to believe Richard was anything other than loyal to King Edward IV, even when their other brother, the Duke of Clarence, rebelled.

Richard's only definite "crime" was losing the Battle of Bosworth. If he'd won, it's possible that by now we'd be telling dark tales of the "evil" Henry Tudor. History is always written by the winners.

Red Rose, White Rose

Whichever head wore the medieval English crown, it was a wobbly fit. It was okay when there was a tough guy on the throne, like Henry V, but when his young son inherited the kingdom, the vultures started circling.

Henry VI preferred books to being king, and worse, he suffered bouts of insanity. Noble families started eyeing his crown.

At the front of the line were rival branches of the royal family of Plantagenet. In the white corner was the House of York, whose badge was a white rose. In the red corner, the House of Lancaster chose a red rose. They'd do anything for a shot at the throne—and they did. The messy, long-running, and blood-spattered results became known as the Wars of the Roses.

Eventually, when Lancastrian Henry Tudor defeated Richard III and married Elizabeth of York, the two flowers were finally brought together as the "Tudor Rose."

Weapons

Richard's battered body had eleven wounds, nine of which were to his head, so he must have lost his helmet. A halberd, a long pole with an axe head *and* a spike on the end of it, had sliced a lump off his skull, and there were signs he'd been stabbed, too, either with a sword or a dagger.

Princes in the Tower

One of the most hideous crimes Richard was accused of was the murder of the young king Edward V and his brother the Duke of York, even though he'd sworn to protect them.

The princes *were* taken to the Tower of London while waiting for Edward's coronation and never seen again, but historians argue as to whether they were actually murdered, and even if they were, if it was really on Wicked Uncle Richard's orders.

In 1674, workmen at the Tower unearthed a strange wooden box. Inside were the skeletons of two children. Could they be the lost princes? Even if it can ever be proven they are, we'll still never know exactly how they died.

Workmen at the Tower of London unearthed a box that contained the skeletons of two children.

His Kingdom for a Horse

You could say that the ex-king's worst enemy hadn't even been born when Richard died. Step forward, Master William Shakespeare!

Shakespeare had a good reason to make Richard into an ogre. Queen Elizabeth I was on the throne, and there had been nearly thirty people who'd had a better claim to be king than her grandfather Henry VII. She needed to make them look as bad as possible, and Will Shakespeare needed royal butts in the seats.

Shakespeare's play gives Richard a hunchback, a limp, a withered hand, and a seriously bad attitude. He schemes and plots, has his brother drowned in a butt of malmsey wine, and then murders the princes in the tower for good measure. Elizabethan audiences adored the evil scoundrel, and he's still as popular as ever today.

Many quotes from *Richard III* have entered our language. We're so familiar with the fictional pantomime villain that it's easy to assume Shakespeare was telling the truth instead of writing a great play to entertain audiences.

William Shakespeare wrote about Richard III as an evil scoundrel.

Bad Man, Good King?

With all his bad press, it's easy to forget Richard was a decent king. He created a special council to keep the peace in the north and a Court of Requests where poor people who couldn't afford lawyers could be heard. Some suspected felons were allowed bail before trial, and he had the law translated from the courtly French into everyday English so folks actually understood it. Best of all, he banned restrictions on the printing and sale of books.

Richard III may have died over 500 years ago, but amazingly, he still has an active fan club!

King in a Parking Lot

After the battle where Richard died, his body was stripped naked and slung over a horse, where it went on public display in Leicester before being buried in the local Greyfriars monastery. When the victorious Henry VII's son, Henry VIII, got rid of the monasteries a few years later, Richard's body disappeared. People said it had been tossed into the River Soar.

In 2013, however, archaeologists unearthed a skeleton in a city parking lot, under a bay next to one marked "R." DNA tests proved the remains were of Richard III. It was covered in battle wounds and had a curved spine, but it's unlikely he would have had an obvious hunchback.

Richard received a king's funeral in March 2015 and now lies beneath a limestone tomb in Leicester Cathedral.

BOSTON TEA PARTY

USA, DECEMBER 16, 1773

Friends! Brethren! Countrymen! That worst of plagues, the detestable tea, is now arrived!

The Boston Tea Party sounds very dainty, but don't be fooled. There were no fancy china cups, no sandwiches, and definitely no cupcakes. Instead, a secret society of American patriots called the Sons of Liberty forcibly boarded ships in Boston Harbor and tossed an entire shipment of tea overboard. Some even disguised themselves (very badly!) as local Mohawk Indians.

They were angry about a new British Act of Parliament which said tea could only be imported to America from Britain (even though it wasn't grown there), creating a monopoly for the despised British East India Company. It was one of many laws the British government kept imposing on the colonists, none of which they'd had any say in making.

In autumn of 1773, seven British ships left Britain, carrying 2,000 chests and 600,000 pounds of tea. Everyone in the

Disguised as Mohawk Indians, the Sons of Liberty tossed an entire shipment of tea overboard.

Around 130 men participated in the Boston Tea Party.

colonies was furious. Colonial merchants, many of whom were smugglers, realized the Tea Act actually made legal tea cheaper, which would put them out of business. Even legal tea importers who weren't part of the East India Company would lose out.

Three ships were persuaded to turn back without unloading their cargo, from Charleston, Philadelphia, and New York, all smuggling towns. The remaining four ships were bound for Boston. Boston was relatively law-abiding, but wasn't going to pay through the nose for being on the level. One ship was stranded at sea, but the other three docked in Boston Harbor.

The royal governor of Boston, Thomas Hutchinson, refused to let the boats either unload or leave without paying a duty, despite 7,000 people turning up for a town meeting. Samuel Adams made a speech, calling the monopoly the equivalent of a tax, and tempers flared. People remembered the five civilian men that British soldiers had killed just three years beforehand in what became

known as the Boston Massacre. Then they remembered this new "tax" would pay for yet more British troops.

That night around 130 men, their faces disguised with grease and coal dust, dumped 342 chests of tea, worth about $1 million in today's money, into Boston Harbor. Although some later admitted they were there that night, we still don't know exactly how many people destroyed the tea, as most "partygoers" kept their involvement a lifelong secret.

The Injured Man

Amazingly, only one man was injured in the incident. The protesters had met at John Crane's house earlier to put on their disguises. They were later shocked when, down in the ship's hold, Crane was hit by a falling tea chest. His compatriots hid the "dead body" under some wood shavings in a nearby carpenter's shop and were freaked out when it "came back to life."

Samuel Adams

Samuel Adams was a veteran of colonial campaigning. He'd fought against the Sugar Act; the Stamp Act, which put a tax on paper goods; and the Townshend Acts, which saw taxes on all sorts of other things.

Although he'd worked to get British troops removed both before and after the Boston Massacre, he was also eager to show the British that Boston was not a lawless mob, and he arranged for the soldiers who'd killed the Boston civilians to get decent representation at their trial.

He'd had numerous run-ins with Boston's governor, Thomas Hutchinson, who was loyal to Great Britain.

When news arrived of ships full of tea at the harbor, Adams called a meeting at the nearby Faneuil Hall. So many people turned up that they had to move to the much bigger Meeting House. They decided to persuade the ship's captains to go home, and they set guards to make sure their cargoes weren't unloaded.

Hutchinson was adamant—those ships weren't going anywhere until they'd coughed up some tax payment.

We don't know if Adams arranged what happened next, but he certainly supported the destruction of the tea and later defended the perpetrators.

Samuel Adams (1722–1803), statesman and one of the founding fathers of the United States.

Thomas Hutchinson

Thomas Hutchinson was American, born in Boston to a wealthy merchant family. He loved his country, but he was also fiercely loyal to Britain. It wasn't a happy combination.

He was deeply unpopular with the mob, who ransacked and then burned down his house, and that was when he was only lieutenant governor. Unfortunately, the man in charge, Francis Bernard, was even less popular than Hutchinson, who got the flack for his decisions.

Things hadn't improved when he became acting governor, though, and it was Hutchinson who was in charge when the Boston Massacre took place.

Two of Hutchinson's sons were responsible for the safe arrival of the tea and the payment of any taxes. It would be them who'd be in trouble if the duty wasn't paid. Hutchinson took a hard line.

The Loyal Nine and the Sons of Liberty

Nine men started meeting together secretly in 1765 to organize protests against a new law called the Stamp Act, which made people pay extra taxes. They were bitter because they didn't even get to have a say. They established the Liberty Tree as a place to meet and tried to scare local British officials so they couldn't enforce the act.

All nine men went on to join the Sons of Liberty, a much larger secret society that organized the Boston Tea Party. Everyone was angry, from respectable citizens to some pretty seedy characters and "wharf rats" who just enjoyed a good fight. Occasionally things got violent. The rallying cry was simple: "No taxation without representation!"

Paying the Excise Man

"Tarring and feathering" was a particularly unpleasant way to spend an afternoon. Victims would be dragged, shrieking and terrified, from their beds, off the street, or from their place of work, and then stripped, doused with hot tar, and rolled in chicken feathers. They'd be paraded around to be laughed at, beaten, whipped, and humiliated.

A "New England Jacket" wasn't usually fatal, as the "tar" used back then wasn't the boiling asphalt we have today, which gets very hot indeed. Tar was a pine resin that melted at lower temperatures, but it still would have scalded the victims. Getting the gooey mess off their blistered skin would have been painful and bloody, but it wasn't always successful as a deterrent. British customs official Captain John Malcolm was tarred and feathered twice and hung from the Liberty Tree. He only apologized for striking shoemaker George Hewes when the mob threatened to cut off his ears.

Tarring and feathering a victim.

The Liberty Tree

Planted in 1646, a giant elm tree on High Street near Hanover Square became a symbol for everything the Sons of Liberty believed in. They hung effigies of British supporters from its boughs, nailed notices to its trunk, decorated it with lanterns, and held meetings in its shadow.

No wonder the British detested what was now known as the Liberty Tree. They cut it down in 1775, but "the Liberty Stump" continued to be a rallying point for many years.

Intolerable!

Back in Britain, people were bewildered, shocked, and exasperated at the protest. King George III was extremely angry, personally advising the prime minister to punish the rebellious colonists.

New laws were passed. The port of Boston was closed until all the lost tea was paid for, town meetings were curbed, town officials were directly appointed from Britain, the justice system was "rigged" in the King's favor, and British soldiers could be lodged more or less wherever the governor chose.

They were called the Coercive Acts. American patriots had another name for them: the Intolerable Acts. Already seething, the Sons of Liberty were edging toward the idea of independence, and less than eighteen months later, they would go to war for it.

A group of patriots meet under the Liberty Tree.

RASPUTIN
RUSSIA, EARLY TWENTIETH CENTURY

Midnight, on a frozen, dark December night in 1916, and there's a knock at the door....

Grigori Rasputin, faith healer and trusted friend of the Russian royal family, has been called to visit a pretty young noblewoman. The mystic goes willingly, unaware his bodyguard has just stopped work.

It's hard to know exactly what happened between Rasputin's last sighting, by a maid watching him leave with dashing Count Felix Yusupov, and the discovery of his body in the frozen Malaya Neva River. All the eyewitness accounts, including those of his murderers, are different. Legends arose that this "devil" of almost superhuman strength just wouldn't die.

Rasputin had been "curing" the tsar and tsarina's son, Alexei, but the public didn't know the boy was even ill. Those who were in on the secret thought Rasputin was a charlatan. His sinister "enchantment" over the royal couple made their flesh crawl, but worse, this crazy peasant was beginning to wield serious power over the way Russia was being run.

Newspapers printed scandals about "dark forces" with cartoons of Rasputin looking even crazier than he did in real life. The only thing that briefly kept him off the front covers was the sinking of the *Titanic*!

Rasputin spoke out against Russia going to war with Germany, saying it would be the end of the monarchy, the Romanovs, and Russian institutions, but even he couldn't stop World War I. The tsar went off to fight, leaving the tsarina in charge. Many worried she'd give Rasputin even more power, and several, including two aristocrats and a politician, decided he had to go.

Newspaper cartoons depicted Rasputin looking like a monster.

In his book, Felix Yusupov claims he and his co-conspirators laced some cakes and sweet wine with cyanide, and then they invited Rasputin to his palace, where they'd created a nice, welcoming room in a basement for him.

The poison should have been enough to kill several men. Whether Rasputin was somehow immune to cyanide, the poison was actually rather weak, or the mystic simply wasn't hungry, we'll never know, but Yusupov says Rasputin kept talking as though nothing had happened.

Yusupov was forced to shoot the unwanted healer at close range. Rasputin fell onto a bearskin rug, and had to be moved quickly to avoid incriminating blood stains. The conspirators, convinced the "evil genius" was dead, went upstairs.

Rasputin woke up. He struggled up the stairs and opened an unlocked door to the courtyard. The conspirators dashed out and shot him again. He fell "dead," but as they approached, the body twitched, so they finished him off with a rubber mallet.

They shot one of Yusupov's dogs as a cover story for the blood stains, and then chucked Rasputin's body in the river, but they forgot to add weights. When his corpse was discovered, it had its

hands in the air as though to escape, which has led to rumors that Rasputin still wasn't dead when his body entered the water.

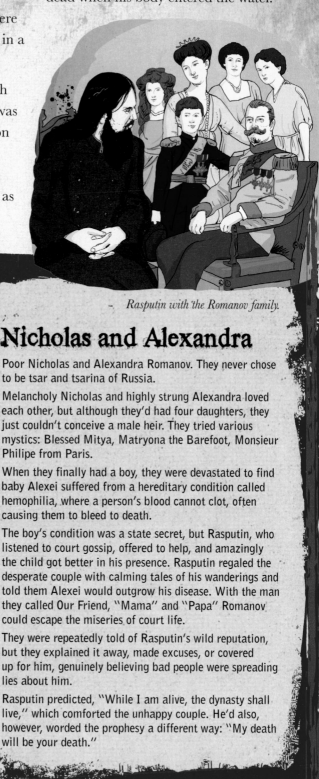

Rasputin with the Romanov family.

Nicholas and Alexandra

Poor Nicholas and Alexandra Romanov. They never chose to be tsar and tsarina of Russia.

Melancholy Nicholas and highly strung Alexandra loved each other, but although they'd had four daughters, they just couldn't conceive a male heir. They tried various mystics: Blessed Mitya, Matryona the Barefoot, Monsieur Philipe from Paris.

When they finally had a boy, they were devastated to find baby Alexei suffered from a hereditary condition called hemophilia, where a person's blood cannot clot, often causing them to bleed to death.

The boy's condition was a state secret, but Rasputin, who listened to court gossip, offered to help, and amazingly the child got better in his presence. Rasputin regaled the desperate couple with calming tales of his wanderings and told them Alexei would outgrow his disease. With the man they called Our Friend, "Mama" and "Papa" Romanov could escape the miseries of court life.

They were repeatedly told of Rasputin's wild reputation, but they explained it away, made excuses, or covered up for him, genuinely believing bad people were spreading lies about him.

Rasputin predicted, "While I am alive, the dynasty shall live," which comforted the unhappy couple. He'd also, however, worded the prophesy a different way: "My death will be your death."

Grigori Rasputin

The one thing everyone agreed on about Rasputin was his eyes. Some believed those haunting, demonic beams could pierce into their very souls; everyone else found them incredibly creepy. The rest of his appearance was peculiar too, with a straggly black beard and thin, lanky hair, parted in the middle and combed to cover a lump his own daughter described as looking like a budding horn!

Peasant life in tzarist Russia was harsh, and Rasputin came from poor stock. He married young and had three children, but he was constantly drunk and starting savage fights. After a particularly nasty bout, onlookers thought he was dead, but Rasputin "came back to life." He had changed.

He became obsessed with religion and started wandering between monasteries, churches, and temples, praying and begging for alms and a place to sleep. He gave up drinking, smoking, and eating meat. To test himself, he didn't wash his undergarments for six months at a time. People called him a holy fool as he waved his arms around, threatening invisible demons.

Amazingly for someone with smelly underpants and crazed looks, and who argued with himself in the street, Rasputin was a hit with the ladies. Society women, countesses, captains' wives—dozens hung on his every word. Men were captivated, too, and Rasputin's circle of followers grew. It was only a matter of time before he was introduced to the sad, desperate tsarina.

Khlysts

Early twentieth-century Russia was falling apart. Searching for "something," some people turned to communism. Others tried ancient religious sects that worshiped pagan gods alongside the saints, or dabbled with bizarre forms of "Christian" worship. These underground movements were banned by the Orthodox Church as heresy, but many whispered that they continued anyway.

The Khlyst sect was particularly extreme. Followers believed if they deliberately committed a sin and then punished themselves harshly for it, it would bring them closer to God. They beat themselves up, literally whipping themselves into a frenzy, and even cut off parts of their bodies in an almost maniacal passion.

Regular Russians thought they were very scary indeed. It is hardly surprising Rasputin was accused of being involved in Khlyst activities.

Setting the Scene ...

It was important Rasputin didn't suspect his forthcoming demise, not least because if his legendary "sixth sense" told him something was wrong, they'd never get him inside the murder room.

The conspirators furnished the basement chamber so it looked sumptuous enough for him to enter willingly. They raided the palace stores for carved chairs, ivory chalices, antique cabinets, and an ancient crucifix made of silver and rock crystal. They added a nice table where the doomed mystic would drink his last cup, and as a finishing flourish, they lay an enormous polar bear skin rug on the floor.

In hindsight, that was probably an error. It's really hard to get blood stains out of white fur....

Secret Burial

Immediately after Rasputin's death, crowds appeared with buckets and jugs, hoping to collect water from the icy river and with it some of his superhuman strength.

He was buried secretly, though his grave in the woods was visited by the tsarina until she was arrested by the Bolsheviks. Rasputin's tomb was found by crowds of revolutionary soldiers. His face had turned black, and he was wearing an icon given to him by the tsarina, who now pleaded for him to be treated with a little decency.

The body was moved in a piano packing case to a garage while they decided what to do with it. He was supposed to be buried secretly a second time by a roadside somewhere unpopulated, but the car that was carrying the corpse got stuck in mud. No one can agree whether the guards decided to incinerate the body in a local boiler shop or build a bonfire, douse the corpse in gasoline, and set fire to it then and there.

The soldiers threw the ashes to the wind, starting a legend that Rasputin passed through all the elements: water, earth, fire, and air.

The chief of police received a telegram from the desperate mayor with an offer to kill Rasputin.

An Offer You Can Refuse ...

In 1913, Rasputin was living the high life in a city called Yalta, where the tsar had just built a palace. The people of Yalta were shocked and upset at Rasputin's behavior around town, and the mayor was worried it made the royal family look bad. When he complained to the tsar, however, he was told to mind his own business.

The distressed mayor sent a telegram to the director of police, offering to kill Rasputin for him. The poor fellow didn't really understand modern technology. He hadn't realized how many pairs of eyes saw "private" messages sent by the newfangled "telegraph" system. If the mystic died, it would be more than obvious not only who had done the job, but who had okayed the hit. The "kind offer" was quietly rejected.

The End of the Romanovs

Not two months after Rasputin's murder, communists known as Bolsheviks staged a revolution, forcing Tsar Nicholas to abdicate.

"Citizen Romanov" and his entire family were moved to the ominous-sounding House of Special Purpose. They were under house arrest—guards fired at the young princesses if they looked out of the window—but while they were alive, they were still possible threats to the new regime.

At midnight on July 16, 1918, the royal family was awoken and told they were being moved. They were ordered to wait in a basement. Alexei was bleeding badly again.

The former tsar and his heir were shot first, and then the tsarina and her daughters were next. Initially, the bullets weren't successful because the children's clothes had jewels sewn secretly into them, which acted like armor, so they were stabbed to death instead.

The executioners doused the bodies in acid and threw them down an old mine, covering them with rubble. They weren't discovered until 1979. After DNA tests proved the skeletons were of the entire royal family, they were given a state funeral.

Maria Rasputin became a lion tamer in the Hagenbeck Wallace Circus.

Maria Rasputin

After escaping to the west, Rasputin's daughter Maria went to the United States, where, after a stint as a cabaret dancer, she became a lion tamer in the Hagenbeck Wallace Circus.

Posters claimed "the daughter of the famous mad monk" could hypnotize the wild beasts with her father's mesmerizing eyes. She even advertised breakfast cereal!

Her performing career ended after she was attacked by a bear.

AMERICAN CIVIL WAR TECH

Hot Air Balloons

Airplanes hadn't been invented by the 1860s, but that didn't stop both the North and the South from using the skies. Hot air balloons were mainly used to see the terrain and to spy on the enemy.

It didn't occur to either side to use camouflage—in fact, their balloons were often brightly colored and carried patriotic slogans. Due to wartime shortages, some Confederate balloons were even made out of dressmaking silk, which led people to whisper that Southern ladies had donated their dresses to make them.

A man named Thaddeus Lowe designed some especially tough balloons for the Union army's "Balloon Corps," but the newfangled technology was mistrusted by crusty old generals, and the balloons were quietly abandoned. One Confederate general was astounded at this, saying it would have been worth the Union keeping their balloons just for the headaches it had caused him trying to keep his troops hidden!

Hot Air Balloon

Angel Glow

After the devastating battle of Shiloh, there were so many wounded soldiers that they couldn't immediately be taken to the hospital. After they'd lain freezing on the swampy battlefield for days, some soldiers started seeing their wounds glowing faintly blue in the dark. When they finally got to the hospital, they healed more quickly and cleanly than their non-luminous buddies, but no one could figure out why. "Angel Glow" became a myth.

In 2001, two teenage high school students doing a science fair project finally discovered the secret. The soldiers had picked up tiny parasitic worms called nematodes from the soil. The nematodes had vomited bacteria to kill their host, but it had eaten its rivals—other bacteria—first!

Germs!

In 1863, Confederate sympathizer Luke P. Blackburn was accused of gathering large amounts of vomit-covered, blood-encrusted bedding from people who'd died from yellow fever. His accusers said he was planning to send them to a hospital full of Union soldiers so they'd catch the disease too. The evil plan wouldn't have worked, as the disease is spread via mosquitoes, not contamination, but the idea of biological warfare had infected the world.

Both sides started experimenting with chemical weapons too, trying to figure out how to fill bullets and bombs with poisonous gases. Luckily, the science was mainly beyond them—for this war at least.

Things That Go Bang in the Night

The mid-nineteenth century saw an explosion in explosives. Confederate naval mines sank around forty Union ships; these would lead to the development of land mines and grenades in later wars.

French army captain Claude-Étienne Minié invented a new bullet—cylindrical rather than round like the old musket balls. *Miniés* (or "minnies," as the troops called them) had a conical point and splayed out at the back when fired, making them both easy to load and lethally accurate.

Richard Gatling's new repeating field gun needed to be cranked by hand, so it wasn't fully automatic. But you still wouldn't want to be in range of its deadly rotating barrels repeatedly shooting at you. He said he'd invented something so deadly people would stop waging war. He was very, very wrong.

Gatling gun designed by the American inventor Dr. Richard J. Gatling in 1861.

The City Class ironclad gunboat USS Baron DeKalb, *constructed for the Union Navy during the American Civil War.*

Ironclads and Submarines

Everyone loved the idea that one day, cannonballs might be able to bounce off of a boat. The first iron-covered ship, called a "turtle," was launched in Korea in 1592—but there was a problem. Armored ships were ridiculously heavy. The wind wasn't strong enough to drive one. Besides, sails could be set on fire or blown to bits.

With the arrival of steam, however, everything changed.

Both sides had their own "ironclads." Because they were being built almost as fast as they were being invented, most looked really weird. One of the strangest has to be the Union's "Monitor" class, which looked like tanks on water, complete with gun turrets. The first battle between ironclads in 1861 meant the days of the wooden warship were over.

Confederate and Union scientists experimented with submarines, but we know very little about them— they kept everything top secret, and records were destroyed. It's thought that around twenty early submarines were sneaking around the waters of America during the war.

Camera

Photography

The American Civil War is the first major conflict to have been widely photographed. Photographers traveled miles, even venturing onto the battlefields. They didn't hold back from snapping the horrors of war, and the folks back home suddenly realized battles weren't quite as romantic as they'd imagined.

Photos couldn't be taken with a simple click. It sometimes took several minutes to "expose" a large glass plate coated with special chemicals, so pictures had to be staged, with everyone standing very still. The photographer then disappeared into his wagon so he could process the plate in the pitch dark using very dangerous chemicals he'd had to mix by hand.

Telegraph and Railroad

The telegraph had been invented a few years before the war. There was already quite a network of cabling, but with the war came 15,000 more miles just for military use. Abraham Lincoln regularly visited the Telegraph Office to catch up on the latest news.

Lincoln also loved the brand-new railroads, vital for transporting troops and supplies. The Union railroads were better connected, but their tracks were vulnerable. Confederate troops used to light fires underneath and then bend them around tree trunks to make "Sherman's neckties."

The Army telegraph setting up the wire during the battle of Fredericksburg, VA. Woodcut by Alfred Waud, December 1862.

INDEX

Numbers in bold indicate that an image of the subject will be found on the page.

GLOSSARY

armada
a fleet of warships. The word is known especially for the Spanish Armada of 1588, which failed in its attempt to invade England

"articulated skeletons"
skeletons which have their bones in a natural arrangement

Aztecs
a warrior tribe of central Mexico

Bolsheviks
meaning "one of the majority" in Russian, the group became the Russian Communist Party

buccaneers
pirates who preyed on Spanish shipping in the Caribbean

Celtic
people from the six Celtic territories: Scotland, Ireland, Wales, Isle of Man, Brittany, and Cornwall

centurions
Roman soldiers in charge of one hundred men

chloroform
a clear liquid with various uses, including as an anaesthetic

crow's nest
a platform at the top of the main mast of a ship, used as a lookout

"Danegeld"
an English tax to protect the country from Viking invaders

forensic science
applies science to law matters, such as criminal cases

freebooters
pirates who pillage and plunder

guillotine
a machine with a heavy blade used for beheading people, invented by Joseph-Ignace Guillotin and used especially in the French Revolution

henna
a flowering plant from which dye is prepared and used in body art and fabric dyeing

hoods
criminals, short for hoodlums

legionnaires
members of legions, large military units, such as in the Roman army

Londinium
the origin of the name of London. It was located on the City of London site

modus operandi
a Latin phrase meaning "method of working"

nobles
members of the nobility, the highest social class

Ottomans
members of the Islamic Ottoman Empire which lasted from 1301-1922

patriots
people who love and defend their country

"Penny Dreadful" storybooks
nineteenth-century cheap, popular stories or comics

Phoenicians
ancient people from Phoenicia, famed as traders and seafarers

pillage
looting or plundering, especially in wartime

privateers
private ship owners who are authorized by government "letters of marque" to attack and capture enemy ships

Prohibition
from 1920-33 in the United States it was illegal to make or sell alcohol

regent
a person who rules a state because the legitimate ruler is a minor, ill, or absent

reincarnation
rebirth of the soul in a new body

shape-shifting
a person or animal who can change into a different form

skulduggery
devious, dishonest behavior or trickery

South Sea Bubble
people who invested in the unprofitable South Sea Company found they had lost everything when the Bubble burst in 1720

swashbuckling
taking part in romantic and heroic adventures

"third estate"
in France's Ancien Régime before the French Revolution, there were three estates: the First Estate (the clergy), the Second Estate (nobility), and the Third Estate (commoners or ordinary people)

torques
a metal necklace or collar, sometimes in a twisted shape

Valhalla
in Norse mythology, a vast hall where Odin housed the chosen dead

Vikings
originated from Scandinavia, famed as seafarers, traders, and raiders

viziers
high and powerful officials in some Muslim countries

ACKNOWLEDGMENTS

Author: Sandra Lawrence

Sandra would like to thank the following
people for their help with this book:

*David Townsend has a rare combination of expertise:
murder, millitary, and maniacs. He was generous with his thoughts
on all three for which I am grateful, in spite of the nightmares.*

*Dr. Dana Huntley's advice on the American chapters was more
valuable than he thinks. I hope he's tickled by the result.*

*My lovely editor Fay Evans kept the faith and always said nice
things about the grimmest stuff. Thank you!*

Illustrator: Bernard Chau

Senior Editor: Fay Evans
Editor: Melissa Brandzel
Designer: Natalie Schmidt
Publisher: Donna Gregory

PICTURE CREDITS:
Page 51, bl Wikimedia
All other images courtesy of shutterstock.